Retail Facilities Maintenance
The Circle of
Management

A 30-Year Experience Management Narrative

AL TIERNEY

WESTBOW
PRESS
A DIVISION OF THOMAS NELSON

WestBow Press books may be ordered through booksellers or by contacting:

WestBow Press
A Division of Thomas Nelson
1663 Liberty Drive
Bloomington, IN 47403
www.westbowpress.com
1-(866) 928-1240

ISBN: 978-1-4497-9822-2 (sc)
ISBN: 978-1-4497-9824-6 (hc)
ISBN: 978-1-4497-9823-9 (e)

Library of Congress Control Number: 2013910694

Printed in the United States of America.

WestBow Press rev. date: 06/20/2013

CONTENTS

Management—Performance

Management—Needs and Results

FOREWORD

During my last twenty-some years in the facility maintenance industry, I can look back at a handful of special moments where I received a gift. Now I'm not referring to a nicely-wrapped package with a bow, but the type of gift that is often overlooked—knowledge. The uniqueness of this gift is that it's everywhere, but it can only be received when we allow ourselves to be open.

Chances are, most of your professional achievements and advancement can be related to the acquisition and practical application of your knowledge.

How many times have you come across an individual whose knowledge and passion for self-improvement can transform your perspective or alter the way you process information? Throughout our lives, most of us can usually think of a few individuals who had a significant impact on our growth, personally and professionally.

I can remember my first meeting with Al Tierney well. He greeted me in their corporate lobby and brought me into a large, glass-walled conference room. As owner of a medium-sized national facility services company, I was excited about the prospects of working for this company and what a positive impact this could have on my business.

During our meeting, Al was providing an overview on department expectations and the principles on which their programs were founded. Through his measured and engaging delivery, Al explained how every component of their locations was managed as well as the management structure in place to support their efforts. This was the most detailed and logical program I had been exposed to date, and there was a moment when I thought, *This makes perfect sense; why doesn't everyone build programs this complete and well thought out?*

After the meeting, Al took me to his desk and gave me two articles on facility management programs he had written almost five years earlier for an industry publication. These articles tied in to the vision discussed during our meeting. As I looked at the publishing date on his articles, I was convinced this man was a visionary, a man operating ahead of his peers.

I left the meeting more excited about the depth of knowledge I had just discovered and the open invitation to learn more than I was about the revenue for my business.

During the months and years that followed, there were many more lessons of the critical components of successful facility management programs. Al had a way of always tying the components into the master strategy of the program in play, a symphony of information that I had not yet been exposed to—and I was all ears.

There were several recurring themes along the way, but the main theme continually placed emphasis on the importance of predictive and preventive maintenance programs and the associated benefits. With a qualified director or manager, these programs can provide considerable savings, predictable expenses (for many years ahead), and operational efficiencies.

Not to be overlooked is the importance of building top—and middle-level management support as the pieces of these programs are developed and strategically pieced together. Having internal management as an ally is key to the life of the program, and not many understand or have more experience in how to navigate this than Al Tierney.

Al has successfully built two such programs at large national companies over the last thirty years. Many of the principles detailed in this book will be of great benefit to the reader. Whether applied in current or future positions, the lessons contained are a key piece of knowledge that will benefit facility professionals throughout their career. Many who will read this may be just getting started or have successful careers. However, you all share a common goal—knowledge.

In closing, I hope readers enjoy the detail provided and are open to receiving a gift from a passionate professional who can always be depended upon, Al Tierney.

Peter Mohrhauser
CEO, Ascential Corporation

Introduction

After nearly forty years of employment—thirty in facilities maintenance management—I am writing this book to foster discussion, development, and deployment of management decisions and direction that affect facilities maintenance of a company's restaurant, retail, or wholesale multi sites. We who labor in this field need to begin a collective whiteboarding process to share and improve upon tried decisions and directions. We need to have a well thought out and effective facilities maintenance narrative that allows those in upper management to better understand the ramifications and benefits of maintaining their point of sale locations. In this way, the directors/managers of facilities maintenance will have greater influence with their companies' facilities maintenance programs.

What is contained in this book is my management experience garnered over a thirty-year career in facilities maintenance with concepts developed and processes tried. Below is a quick synopsis of my work history.

My last day as the director of facilities maintenance for Company A was December 21, 2012. My working resume is shown in Appendix A.

Prior to facilities management, there were a couple other management experiences that I would like to mention. First, there was my role as the resident engineer on an Illinois Department of Transportation highway and bridge construction project. Next, I started the civil engineering department for a village in the western suburbs of Chicago.

I graduated from the University of Dayton in April of 1973 with a civil engineering degree. My first position was with a large engineering firm in downtown Chicago. This company had many disciplines of engineering services. I worked in the civil engineering land development department. I started preparing the engineering drawings for single-family and multi-family planned unit developments. This entailed the grading plans, the municipal utilities plans, the detention or retention plans, and the right-of-way plans for the roadways and sidewalks.

This company reassigned me to the above-mentioned highway and bridge project. After the completion of this project, I left to begin work as the village engineer for a western suburb of Chicago; I was their first in-house engineer. As such, I established the engineering procedures for the land developments.

After two more working positions as director of engineering and transportation engineer with two separate companies, I became interested in real estate development. I enrolled in a Realtor-in-training program. I took this class successfully, and it led me to look for real estate positions within corporations.

My first corporate real estate job was with Company B. I started out as a new store project manager. As such, I found the site within a city where the company wanted to place a new branch, coordinated the development of the construction plans, and then oversaw the construction of the branch. After a year, I was asked to start a facilities maintenance area for the company. A year later, I was working full-time as its facilities maintenance manager.

I was with this company for more than nineteen years. After about ten years, the operations department manager came to me and asked me to develop a predictive and preventative maintenance program for the company. This was accomplished with the help of two project managers. Details about this program will be discussed later.

After eight years of administering the predictive and preventative maintenance program, I left this company to start my own business. This company was Regal Alliance. I wanted to share with other companies the principles of a predictive and preventative maintenance program. After September 11, 2001 it was difficult to get business, so I reentered the corporate workforce. I began working for Company A.

The real estate vice president stated that the company wanted to start a predictive and preventative facilities maintenance program. I was hired to develop the very facilities maintenance program that I was wired to do for a company that had a great need for it.

I have had great management opportunities in my career. My first boss used to say, "Boys, we're cutting like a diamond." What he meant was that we were facing the challenge in front of us with high energy and precision.

My second-to-last boss used to say, "You can't manage what you don't see." What he meant was that you needed reports to show the facts that would let you know how your performance matched the goals. I will share some thoughts on top-level management's role with its company's facilities maintenance and do the same with middle-level management's role. With first-level management, real estate facilities maintenance project managers, and vendors project management, I will get specific with management processes and responsibilities. Finally, the operations department's needs and results expectations will be discussed. All of this will be done so that you will see the energy, passion, and facts needed to perform facilities maintenance well at whatever stage of management you may be.

A qualifier needs to be put forth here. There are different types of facilities maintenance: factory plants with machinery that have in-house maintenance staffs; stores in mall settings that do not typically have capital improvements issues (i.e., roofs, parking lots, HVAC, etc.); and outsourced maintenance staffs, etc. My background in over thirty years of facilities maintenance has mainly been with stand-alone buildings that included all the maintenance concerns. The material in this book will most directly correlate with my experiences.

1

MANAGEMENT CONCEPTS

There are many books on management, so I don't want to get bogged down with management concepts. But I think we need a minimal scope of management to better grasp how it functions in the world of facilities maintenance.

I searched for the term *management,* and I was sent to Wikipedia. There was a ten-page printed response. The following are portions of this response:

[1]"Management in all business and organizational activities is the act of getting people together to accomplish desired goals and objectives using available resources efficiently and effectively.

Management comprises planning, organizing, staffing, leading or directing, and controlling an organization or effort for the purpose of accomplishing a goal. Resourcing encompasses the deployment and manipulation of human resources, financial resources, technological resources, and natural resources."

"Management,"
Wikipedia, accessed January 7, 2013.
http://www.wikipedia.com/management.

[2]"Basic functions—management operates through various functions that are often classified as planning, organizing, staffing, leading or directing, controlling or monitoring, and motivation.

Planning is deciding what needs to happen in the future (today, next week, next month, next year, over the next five years, etc.) and generating plans for action.

Organizing is the implementation of a pattern of relationships among workers that makes optimum use of the resources required to enable the successful carrying out of plans.

Staffing includes performing job analysis, recruitment, and hiring for appropriate jobs.

Controlling and monitoring entail checking progress against plans.

Motivation is also a function of management. Without motivation, employees cannot work effectively. If motivation does not take place in an organization, employees may not contribute to the other functions (that are usually set by top-level management).

There are some basic roles to consider. Interpersonal roles involve coordination and interaction with employees. Informational roles involve handling, sharing, and analyzing information. Decisional roles require decision-making.

Management skills can be political (used to build a power base and establish connections), conceptual (used to analyze complex situations), interpersonal (used to communicate, motivate, mentor, and delegate), diagnostic (the ability to visualize the most appropriate response to a situation), and technical (expertise in one's particular functional area)."

"Management,"
Wikipedia, accessed January 7, 2013.
http://www.wikipedia.com/management.

[3]"Top-level managers consist of those on a board of directors, presidents, vice-presidents, CEOs, etc. They are responsible for controlling and overseeing the entire organization. They develop goals, strategic plans, and company policies and make decisions on the direction of the business. In addition, top-level managers play a significant role in the mobilization of outside resources and are accountable to the shareholders and general public. The role of the top management can be summarized as follows:

- Top management lays down the objectives and broad policies of the enterprise.

- It issues necessary instructions for preparation of departmental budgets, procedures, schedules, etc.
- It prepares strategic plans and policies for the enterprises.
- It appoints the executive for middle-level (i.e., departmental) managers.
- It controls and coordinates the activities of all the departments.
- It is also responsible for maintaining contact with the outside world.
- It provides guidance and direction.
- The top management is also responsible to the shareholders for the performance of the enterprise.

Middle-level managers consist of general managers, branch managers, and departmental managers. They are accountable to the top management for their departments' functions. They devote more time to organizational and directional functions. Their roles can be emphasized as executing organizational plans in conformance with the company's policies and the objectives of top management. They define and discuss information and policies from top management to lower management, and most importantly, they inspire and provide guidance to lower-level management toward better performance.

Some of their functions are as follows:

- designing and implementing effective group and intergroup work and information systems
- defining and monitoring group-level performance indicators
- diagnosing and resolving problems within and among work groups
- designing and implementing reward systems that support cooperative behavior

First-level managers consist of supervisors, section leads, forepersons, etc. They focus on controlling and directing. They usually have the responsibility of assigning employees tasks, guiding and supervising employees on day-to-day activities, ensuring quality and quantity production, making recommendations and suggestions, upchanneling employee problems, etc. First-level managers are role models for employees who provide basic supervision, motivation, career planning, and performance feedback."

"Management,"
Wikipedia, accessed January 7, 2013.
http://www.wikipedia.com/management.

Let's now look at the circle of management that makes up a corporation's facilities maintenance program.

II

THE CIRCLE OF MANAGEMENT

Direction
Company President
Chief Financial Officer
Chief Operations Officer

Application
VP of Real Estate
Director of Facilities Maintenance
Facilities Maintenance Project Managers

Needs and Results
Zone's VPs of Operations
Zone's Controllers
District Management
Store Managers

Performance
Vendors and contractors:
Roofing
Parking lots
HVAC equipment
Passage doors and windows
Garage doors
Electrical panels and systems
Lighting

General contracting
    Plumbing: fixtures, municipal utilities, fire sprinklers
    Exterior walls
    Floors, interior walls, and ceilings
Signage
Janitorial
Landscaping and snow removal
Security systems

The management decisions revolve clockwise from direction, to needs, to performance, to results, which get back to direction. Application is the center of the circle, receiving the direction, receiving and knowing the needs, selecting the vendors and contractors, providing the application for the performance, and receiving the feedback on results and feedback from direction.

Communication exists both ways between direction and application, needs and application, performance and application, results and application, and finally again with direction and application. The engine of the circle is application. The facilities maintenance information, processes, communication, direction, and oversight emanate from this management hub.

Direction, needs, and results contain the business unit, and application and performance make up the provided facilities maintenance service.

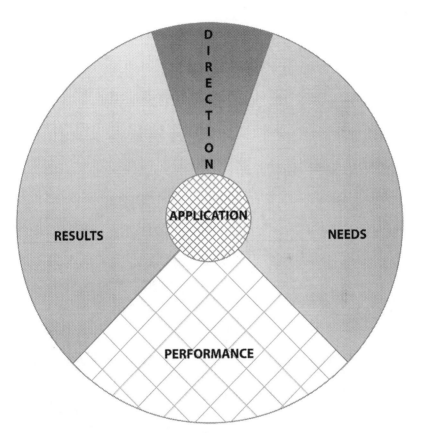

The Circle of Management

III

TOP-LEVEL MANAGEMENT— PRESIDENT, COO AND CFO

The president, chief economic officer, and chief operations officer of a company have many departmental requests for approval to proceed with program or system improvements. Each sponsor of these improvements is sure that his or her department will perform much better and the company will greatly benefit from them. Consider the many departments that support the business and vie for program or system improvements funding:

- IT
- real estate
- purchasing
- manufacturing
- supply chain
- human resources
- customer services
- marketing
- legal services
- environmental services
- loss prevention
- security

The problem is that the company does not have unlimited funds to approve all these programs or system recommended improvements.

There has to be oversight and constraint for all these proposed improvements. I read in a book by John Maxwell, entitled, 'Developing the Leader Within You' where he wrote "You have to say no to the good in order to say yes to the best." He was discussing our busy lives and how we can't do everything. We need to say no to some good activities so we have time to do the best activities. This principle certainly applies here as well. Given the annual budget that a company has established for program or system improvements, what are the most vital improvements that can be approved? Not only is there the issue of how much money is available and what the costs of the proposed improvements are, but there is also the issue of the company direction and what proposed improvements are positioned to that true north. There is the issue of manpower—how much human capital we can apply to proposed improvements.

The pressures are enormous within a large corporation to provide direction on the company mission. What is it? How are we going to attain it? What does each department within the organization need to provide to ensure success? How are departments best suited to work with one another to obtain success? What improvements are mission critical?

The company is in business to make money. Meeting and hopefully exceeding expected profit margins is the bottom line for the corporation's top-level management team. Top-level management has its finger on the pulse of the daily sales and expenses and knows if the company is performing as projected. Expenses need to be controlled so profits can be maximized. However, sometimes there is a clarion call to control expenses. In these times, the proposed improvements can be put on hold, funding for approved budgets are reduced, and in severe cases, there is a reduction in the workforce.

The economy will greatly affect the preparation of a company's annual budget and thereby the spending habits. A downturn in the economy (that directly affects the company's sales performance in a negative way) will put great pressure on top-level management to make internal spending corrections that could enable the company to remain profitable.

In this business environment, the company's facilities maintenance program exists. Maintenance costs are considered a loss to the bottom line of profitability. Hopefully, there is high regard for the company brand and the ultimate boss, the customer, that drives management to the conclusion that maintenance of its business assets is of utmost importance. By business assets, I mean the properties and buildings where the businesses are located. The pressures are such that top-level management will be tempted to reduce facilities maintenance spending or keep it underfunded.

In the final analysis, members of top-level management have the position that determines how much money the company is willing to spend on facilities maintenance. They will listen to their region or zone VPs of operation, the VP of real estate, and hopefully, the director or manager of facilities maintenance for input on the need for facilities maintenance. They themselves, in many instances, came from the operations side of the business and have their own preconceived thoughts on the facilities maintenance needs of the company. They also travel often to the stores and see for themselves how the stores are being maintained. The company also has many meetings with district managers and store managers to get their input on many issues; facilities maintenance is somewhere on that list.

Corporate facilities maintenance is very visible to everyone in the organization. However, we are not all processing the same conclusions. We have all heard the statement, "Perception is reality." It is amazing the varied perceptions that everyone will have on facilities maintenance. Let's face it—members of top-level management have many aspects of the business on their minds, and they are not facilities maintenance experts. Who do they get their input from regarding facilities maintenance, therefore helping them make their conclusions concerning it? Are they the right conclusions? How anxious are they to hear from the facilities maintenance experts to ascertain the complete overall picture of their maintenance programs and how effective they are in the eyes of the boss?

Companies place a high value on their marketing programs. They do all they can to get or entice customers to come through the front doors of their stores. They are very conscious of wanting to create a brand experience—products and/or services that separate them from their competition. With all this emphasis to get the customer—the boss—to come to their store and have a positive experience, you would expect that maintenance of the stores would be highly regarded to better assure a return visit by the customer.

The president will provide the final approval for the corporate facilities maintenance program spending. The chief financial officer needs to fully support the needed maintenance program, because she or he approves and signs off on the spending. Input from the chief operations officer and the vice presidents of operations is extremely important. The vice president of real estate needs to be knowledgeable of the facilities maintenance concerns and fully support the appropriate maintenance program response. The director or manager of facilities maintenance needs to be the expert. This person needs to be knowledgeable of the conditions of the existing stores: knowhow to address the maintenance needs; adequate staff to coordinate, as needed, the implementation of the building components maintenance, repairs, and replacements; and the professional capability to develop a network of vendors that are trustworthy, are cost-competitive, and deliver quality workmanship.

The main group of people who will decide the facilities maintenance activity for the company consists of the president, the chief financial officer, the chief operations officer, the operations region or zone vice presidents, the vice president of real estate, and the director or manager of facilities maintenance.

IV

MIDDLE-LEVEL MANAGEMENT— REAL ESTATE AND OPERATIONS VPs

The vice president of real estate will typically have responsibilities to manage new store construction, existing store reimages or refresh projects, the leased stores portfolio of leases and facilities maintenance. She or he will also oversee all the computer systems used within the real estate department and the invoicing processing and spending for all real estate activity.

It is most likely that this position will not be filled with a facilities maintenance professional or expert. Hopefully, the position is filled with a person who understands the facilities maintenance needs and fully supports having a facilities maintenance professional to provide input on what the company's maintenance needs are and how the maintenance program should be managed. He or she is then able to give the facilities maintenance director or manager full reign to implement the maintenance program. The facilities maintenance director or manager needs to keep the vice president of real estate informed of the activities within the facilities maintenance program. These updates need to be at a minimum on a monthly basis.

The vice president of real estate must be an advocate of the facilities maintenance program. He or she is, in most cases, a member of the president's staff meetings. These high-level meetings will include discussion of departmental activity and spending. The vice president of real estate needs to be well-versed on the facilities maintenance program activities and spending to give accurate information at these meetings and on occasion to defend them.

Political correctness can set in at the top—and middle-level management areas concerning spending trends. Facilities maintenance can become an easy target to reduce maintenance programs and spending. There will be occasions when the vice president of real estate needs to support the necessary facilities maintenance requirements of the company's point of sales properties and recommend that maintenance cuts not be considered. At the minimum, this person should give information on why recommended maintenance cuts are not advisable from a real estate perspective.

The vice president of real estate will also be involved with the operations regions or zones vice presidents. She or he will have a direct line of communication with these people. They will provide direct feedback from operations leadership on the status of the facilities maintenance program. Operations has many meetings: district-wide store managers' meetings, region or zone district staff meetings, region or zone store managers' and district staff meetings, and an annual meeting of store managers and district staff from all regions or zones. Even though there could be over a thousand stores, the communication among operations is usually quick and accurate. If there are concerns with the performance of the facilities maintenance program, the vice president of real estate is going to hear about it—and quickly.

The operations department is the facilities maintenance customer. What maintenance do they want done to their stores? There are two distinct types of maintenance responsibilities for the stores. One is custodial maintenance and repair work; the other is facilities management. The following excerpts are from an article entitled "Corporate Maintenance and the P&L Report" that was published in the Professional Retail Store Maintenance magazine in April of 2002. This article was written by Dave DiCarlo and me. A copy of this article is attached in Appendix B.

[4]Custodial maintenance and repair work is the day-to-day housekeeping needed to properly run a business. These

---

[4]   Al Tierney and Dave Dicarlo, "Corporate Maintenance and the P&L Report," *Professional Retail Store Maintenance,* April 2002, 40.

responsibilities range from general cleanliness, weekly landscape and lawn work, routine checks to ensure security systems are working and operating equipment is functioning properly, and smaller repairs to the building's plumbing fixtures, parking lots and sidewalks.

Facilities management work effectively and efficiently preserves the esthetics, waterproofing, integrity and safety of the property, such as the landscaped areas, the parking lots, all sidewalks, stairs and landings and the building itself.

Where the facilities maintenance program is budgeted along with where the spending is being reported is a huge concern. This issue will be discussed in more detail when we look at the director or manager of facilities maintenance responsibilities as they relate to what facilities maintenance level of service the company wants. The referenced article covers these issues in greater detail.

Suffice it to say, if the facilities maintenance program is tracked at the store level and is applied to its profit and loss statement, then the company has put a lot of power in the hands of the store manager and district manager, thereby allowing the company assets to deteriorate. Maintenance expenditures are considered a loss and reduce the bottom-line profits. This in turn will affect store manager's and district manager's annual bonuses. I raise this management issue here, but we will discuss it in greater detail later.

V

FIRST-LEVEL MANAGEMENT— DIRECTOR/MANAGER FACILITIES MAINTENANCE

Now we come to the management of the application of the company's facilities maintenance program. This program should be managed by an experienced person who is familiar with the challenges to be met, issues to be solved, communication to be had, workload to be completed, funds to be managed, vendors to be utilized, staff that needs to be in place, data to be tracked, and reports that provide the results. At the minimum, this position needs to be a director or manager of facilities maintenance. This position should report directly to the VP of real estate and needs to be equal to the other director or manager positions that report to the VP of real estate: design, construction, accounting, leasing transactions, and new store development.

One day, I was suddenly thrust into facilities maintenance. Company B did not have a facilities maintenance area. The real estate new store manager had asked a more seasoned new store real estate project manager to start the company's facilities maintenance area. He was allowed to say, "I want to remain as a new store project manager." The real estate manager then called in the junior member of his new store project manager's team—me. I was not given an option. "You will start this company's facilities maintenance area," he told me.

I was in my early thirties and married with three small children. I accepted the challenge for family preservation. I shared with my wife, Cathy, that evening that I was the facilities maintenance project manager for the company. I had the dual real estate project management role until facilities maintenance oversight became a full-time job. My passion morphed from new store development to the maintenance of the stores. My journey had begun.

I was in this position for more than nineteen years. It was during this period that I had the opportunity with two FMPMs to develop a predictive and preventative facilities maintenance program. I will go into this development further later in the book. It was a great development to be part of and to put into action. The results were well received by the operations department.

Again, I had the opportunity to develop a predictive and preventative facilities maintenance program when I was hired to do so for the Company A. This time, there were about six times the number of stores, and there was an immediate need to address the deferred maintenance. It was exciting to put in place national and regional maintenance programs that would raise the level of maintenance service. This work assignment was a great incubator for the proof of the results of the predictive and preventative program that we developed at Company B. Our team of five facilities maintenance people had great rapport with customers and responded quickly to address their needs. The four FMPMs who assisted me were (and are) exceptional. Their passion for serving the customer right the first time made my job easy and assured our efforts would be successful.

The director or manager of facilities maintenance should have the mission of keeping the existing fleet of stores in a maintenance condition that is close to that of the new stores. In this way, the company brand is maintained. This is very important today due to the competition that exists for all businesses to succeed. All businesses want to impress the boss—the customer. They want to create a positive experience each and every time the boss enters their restaurant or store. Therefore, the level of maintenance service is important, and an expert is needed to administer the application of the maintenance program.

Is facilities maintenance a necessary evil or a necessary good? It is disappointing to realize that many top-level management personnel would answer this question with the former choice. A good director or manager of facilities maintenance will operate from the position of answering this question with the latter choice. It is her or his duty to convince (or never stop trying to convince) top-level management and middle management of this fact.

In some jobs, this next statement is true, but in being a good director or manager of facilities maintenance, this statement is absolutely true: "You have to risk losing your job to make a difference in your job." There are so many negative preconceived notions about facilities maintenance that it is not possible to be indifferent in this position. One must do what has to be done to be successful in addressing the maintenance needs of the company. There will be difficult discussions with top—and middle-level management. But like I used to tell these people, "I am being paid to be the director of facilities maintenance, and I wouldn't be doing my job if I didn't advise you as I am."

There is so much activity in facilities maintenance that there is no way to be effective without having a detailed approach to this job. A cavalier approach to tracking a project, databasing the completed project information, filing a project, processing the invoicing, and communicating with the customer is not acceptable.

As I stated in the introduction, I had a boss who constantly said, "You can't manage what you don't see." Oh, how true this statement is. The better you see, the better you can gauge your progress. You are conscious of the activity and able to respond to all questions. It is better to have reports in place that answer all the questions.

There are many approaches to approving vendors or contractors to be able to perform maintenance improvements. The unit code or unit cost management approach is extremely beneficial for being able to respond cost-effectively, quickly, and uniformly.

The life cycles of the building components is a necessary point of knowledge. The actual life cycles of the building components that you are responsible to maintain must be known. In this way, you can better predict the repair or replacement needs. The life cycle of a building component and where in years the actual building component is needs to be known by the FMPM when dealing with a maintenance issue.

The issue of repairing or replacing needs to be evaluated each and every time a maintenance project presents itself. Having a tool and information to assist with this decision is necessary due to the frequency of its determination.

The facilities maintenance annual spending should be summarized in the cost per square foot for all the building's total square foot area. This figure is determined by dividing the total maintenance cost by the total square foot area of the buildings served. The average square foot area of a store times this rate per square foot will provide the average facilities maintenance annual spending per store. This allows the maintenance program spending issue to address the level of maintenance service discussion versus questions about specific maintenance projects.

The maintenance program that best addresses what the boss wants is the predictive and preventive maintenance program. In this way, the existing fleet of stores stays close to the new stores in functionality and appearance.

I briefly went into some aspects of management used by a director or manager of facilities maintenance. Let's now explore the aspects of management of a director or manager of facilities maintenance in detail.

A. Purpose of Facilities Maintenance—The Why

The purpose of Facilities Maintenance is to maintain, repair, and replace restaurants', stores' or warehouses' building components and equipment as needed. The primary building components are roofing, parking lots, HVAC equipment, overhead doors, man doors, windows, electrical systems, lighting, signage, plumbing, exterior walls, interior floors, walls, and ceilings. Equipment for the site will vary upon usage. All of these components and equipment will have their maintenance needs addressed for the following reasons:

- for the safety and security of our teammates and customers
- for the operational effectiveness of the use or purpose of the building components

- for customers' perspectives of our stores' operations
- for our company's brand—older stores similar to new stores in appearance and function
- for enabling us to continue to do business at our stores

The director or manager of facilities maintenance will want to provide the necessary company facilities maintenance to meet these purposes. To come up short in meeting these needs stings and is very visible. We will hear on occasion from top—and middle-level management that the company is in business to make money and can't afford to spend the funds necessary to do all of the recommended maintenance. We then do a couple of things. First, we stretch the dollars available to do as much as we are able. Second, we try to recover the reduced funding when the business's profits are in order.

You have to pick your moments, but there are times when the director or manager of facilities maintenance has to have a sense of duty to push his or her company to reach for the highest level of maintenance service that is attainable given budget submittals.

B. Services Provided by Facilities Maintenance—The What

Facilities Maintenance should provide the following maintenance services:

- safety of the building components
- security needs for the property
- operational effectiveness of the building components
- weatherproofing of the building envelop
- appearance of the property and building exterior and interior

These are the services that a facilities maintenance area will have responsibility for. There are many approaches to providing these services. What follows is a discussion on how these services are provided.

C. Performance of Facilities Maintenance—The How

How will facilities maintenance be performed? There are three main classifications of facilities maintenance approaches:

1. Fix it when it breaks
2. Predictive and preventative
3. A combination of 1 and 2

The first two choices are the guard rails of facilities maintenance. The first choice has as its aim to spend as little money as possible. On a spreadsheet of costs, this will look good. The downside is looking at the results of the maintenance services provided. How are the building components holding up? Is the needed security provided to the stores? Are the building components operating as they are intended to? Is the building envelop properly weatherproofed? Does the appearance of the property and store invite the boss to select your store over his or her other choices? Does the interior condition of the store promote positive morale for the company personnel who work there? Although the reduced maintenance cost initially looks inviting, the deferred maintenance will provide ongoing negative effects, and eventually, the older stores will require a large sum of money to address the years of neglect.

When you visit a store or stores that have operated under this choice of maintenance for a long time—say, twenty years or more—it is shocking. You are left wondering how this company's sales location could be in such deplorable condition. After you find out it is a corporate culture of maintenance being accounted for at each site in its profit and loss statement, you shake your head in disbelief that this process is perpetuated, given what it does to the condition of the store(s).

The second choice has as its aim to provide the required ongoing maintenance needs that best meet the purpose of facilities maintenance and do so in an ongoing, cost-conscious manner. This choice will institute facilities maintenance management tools to optimize the dollars spent and provide the maintenance needed to guarantee that the company brand exists for stores new and old.

The only way this choice of maintenance can exist is for the facilities maintenance expenditures to *not* be assigned on each store's profit and loss statement. Top—and middle-level management have to be cognizant that deferred maintenance is allowed to run rampant with facilities maintenance assigned to each store's profit and loss statement. Management takes a stand and doesn't allow the company's assets to be held hostage to store and district staff bonuses.

The third choice has many derivatives, but it will take some of the concepts of 'fixing it when it breaks' and some of the concepts of 'predictive and preventative'. This approach tries to put on the scales the cost concern with the purpose concern and be efficient in finding a balance. Note that any maintenance program that is less in scope than the predictive and preventative program has inherent deferred maintenance.

It is here that I would like to introduce the concept of the level of maintenance service. We need to assess a grade to the maintenance services being provided given the purpose of facilities maintenance. I put forth the following grades of the level of maintenance service:

A. *Excellent:* the purpose of facilities maintenance fully met
B. *Good:* the purpose of facilities maintenance met on a building component replacement basis (capital) but not on a repair basis (expense)
C. *Below boss acceptability:* both capital and expense expenditures are not keeping up with the life cycle needs of the building components
D. *Deplorable:* budget cuts have the capital and expense expenditures significantly below what is needed
F. *Frightening:* there is not much of a facilities maintenance program

The more predictive and preventative the facilities maintenance program is, the higher the level of maintenance service and the lower the deferred maintenance. Conversely, the more the program aims to fix it when it breaks, the lower the level of maintenance service and the higher the deferred maintenance.

By keeping good data on the maintenance spending for all stores and dividing this total by the total square footage of all the stores, you derive the cost per square foot of maintenance spending. The director or manager of facilities maintenance should be able to know or approximate the cost per square foot for each of the level of maintenance service grades shown above. This information should be known by the top—and middle-level management personnel involved with facilities maintenance. In this way, they are better informed of the options and costs of facilities maintenance programs for their company.

My experience has shown that the "fix it when it breaks" approach to facilities maintenance can grade out anywhere between a *C* and an *F* depending on the proper determination of replacement of a building component rather than continually repairing it beyond its life cycle (see repair and replacement guidelines for further explanation). The predictive and preventative approach can provide a grade of *A* if all the building components are included. The combination of the two approaches will most likely grade out between a *B* and a *D*, depending on the extent of building components that have a life cycle replacement program.

These three different classifications of facilities maintenance will each get their own chapter to better define them and explain how they work. First, however, I would like to cover aspects of management for the director or manager of facilities maintenance so we can better understand the discussions of these three classifications of facilities maintenance.

D. Facilities Maintenance Accounting

See "Corporate Maintenance and the P&L Report" in Appendix B for a full discussion on this matter. There are two types of maintenance that impact the multi sites of a company. One is custodial, and the other is facilities management. Custodial maintenance and repair work consist of the day-to-day housekeeping needed to properly run a business. Facilities management works effectively and efficiently to preserve the esthetics, waterproofing, integrity, and safety of the property.

The facilities maintenance director or manager needs to be aware of the custodial line items for spending and the total annual spending of these items, even though this maintenance work is approved by the appropriate district and the impacted store manager administers the work that gets done. What is the annual cost per square foot for this maintenance type? In other words, what is the total custodial spending of all the stores divided by the total square footage of all the stores? This cost per square foot will be added to the facilities management cost per square foot to get the company's total annual maintenance cost per square foot.

When I was with Company B, there were occasions when the accounting department would visit with me during the budgeting process and want to reduce the maintenance funds. I reminded them that we were only spending one dollar a square foot for the company's facilities maintenance programs, including capital and expense. I urged them to consider a home that has two thousand square feet and is fifteen years old. Would it be within reason that this homeowner might spend $2,000 for the annual maintenance of the property and home? They then realized the efficiency of our company's facilities maintenance program and approved the budget as is to maintain our commercial business branches. This cost per square foot is low due to the average square foot area of a store and the clean nature of the use of the building. The majority of the building was the storage of products sold.

The custodial costs should be applied to each store's P&L report. The facilities maintenance costs should not be applied to each store's P&L report. Company A, where I was the director of facilities maintenance, had home office-funded programs set up by the CFO for our facilities maintenance program. The maintenance programs included capital programs (roofing, parking lots, overhead doors, HVAC, signs, general maintenance, and special projects that were defined as projects that had multiple maintenance issues and costs that were much higher than individual building component maintenance issue costs; general maintenance was defined as building components' needs other than those listed above) and expense programs (roofing, parking lots, overhead doors, HVAC, signs, lighting, electrical panels, electrical branch, and general maintenance).

The costs hit the zone spending ledger but did not impact the store or district reports. Consequently, their bonuses were not impacted by the facilities management spending.

This is critical to having a facilities management program that can properly address the maintenance needs to the multi sites' building components. There is no possibility of having a predictive and preventive maintenance program if all maintenance spending is put toward each location's P&L report. If all maintenance is applied to the site's P&L report, then maintenance direction has been given to the district staff and store managers. This situation allows the company's assets to deteriorate in the interests of individual bonuses. Companies should maintain their bonus structures but not allow their sites maintenance needs to be impacted because of them.

The best solution would be to have facilities management spending be included in a site's fixed rent cost. Simply add the known facilities management annual cost per square foot for the desired level of maintenance service to the annual cost per square foot of rent for each site.

E. Customers—Operations: Region or Zone VPs and Controllers, District Staff, and Store Managers

The store managers are part of the largest group of customers and are the front line for our efforts. We need to present to the controllers and district staff (district managers and assistant district managers) a clear delineation of what maintenance work is performed at the store level and what maintenance work is performed through the real estate facilities maintenance (REFM) area. Then the district staff members relay this information to their store managers.

Store managers spend a lot of time at the store. If they are aware that there are home office funds for the maintenance of the major building components, they are much more likely to contact their real estate facilities maintenance project managers (FMPM) for maintenance needs of these building components. We welcome their communication. We want to service them and keep the property and store well-maintained so that they will have more customers, be better able to service those customers, and have a greater likelihood of the customers returning to their stores.

The operations people are the hardest-working people within the company. They put in many hours and face severe pressures to not only be profitable, but also ahead of other regions or zones, districts, and stores. We always considered it a great opportunity to be in meetings with our customers and have a spot on the agenda to discuss their maintenance concerns. They really appreciate the effort by anyone from corporate to meet them on their turf and hear them out.

We established the Customer Bill of Rights so that our FMPMs and vendors remained focused on the needs of the store managers.

Customer Bill of Rights

1. The ultimate customer is the store manager.
2. All contractors, technicians, and vendors who go to a store as directed by the real estate department will treat all store personnel with respect.
   a. They will answer all of the store manager's questions.
   b. They will introduce themselves to the store manager when performing work at the store.
   c. They will explain to the store manager what work they are there to inspect and perform.
   d. Each day that concludes with work performed, the contractor, tech, or vendor will explain what work was performed.
   e. Upon completion of the work, the contractor, vendor, or tech will walk the work site with the store manager, explain the work performed, and submit a sign in/sign out sheet to them for their review and signature.
3. FMPMs will submit the scope of work (when available) to the store manager prior to the contractor, tech, or vendor coming to the store to do the work.

4. Store managers will be real estate facilities maintenance "eyes and ears" for work performed at their stores.
   a. They will keep tabs on work performed as best they can.
   b. They will review sign in/sign out sheets from the contractors, techs, and vendors and approve them or contact the FMPM to indicate why they can't. They should be able to sign the form if the work conforms to the approved quote and purchase order, the work is done correctly, and the work site is properly cleaned and all debris properly disposed of.
5. Store managers will not solicit additional work to be added to the approved quote or purchase order. If they want additional work, they need to contact their FMPM to get approval.

At my last company, there was one assistant district manager per district who had operations responsibility for her or his stores' maintenance. We had a lot of contact with the assistant district managers. There were nearly 100 of them. There was a wide range of maintenance concerns exhibited within this group. We wanted to have good working relationships with all of them. We tried to let them know that we wanted to address any of their facilities maintenance concerns to the best of our ability. A limited budget would be the only reason we couldn't address their "should-do" requests. If communication was not beneficial with a store manager, the assistant district manager would be contacted to help alleviate the differences. This aid was almost always effective.

District Managers had anywhere from twelve to thirty-six store managers plus their assistant district managers reporting to them. The pressure on district managers to generate sales is enormous, and the competition among their peers is legendary. We jumped at the opportunity to serve them. If they had a store manager district meeting and requested our presence, we went. What a great opportunity to serve the district manager and meet our customers face-to-face. The interaction in these groups would be lively, to say the least, but nonetheless, these were great meetings. The result was a better understanding of their needs and how we serviced them.

They greatly appreciated corporate personnel coming out to meet them on their turf.

There are true emergencies, and then there are what I call quasi-emergencies. Any time a VP or controller of a region or zone called and requested that some maintenance work be performed at one of his or stores, we jumped. These projects took on an emergency nature—quasi-emergencies. It didn't matter if these projects were "should-do" or "would like to do."

F. Facilities Maintenance Staffing

Suffice it to say, your facilities maintenance staff will be lean. When I retired at the end of 2012, I had four FMPMs to service more than two thousand stores. *This book will primarily address how maintenance is managed with these numbers and minimal in-house computer systems capability.*

If you are going to have minimal FMPMs, you better be darn careful which ones you hire. Allow me to highlight the negative and positive attributes of a FMPM.

Negative Attributes

- self-absorbed with his or her perceived abilities and way of doing things
- does not respect authority
- wants to do things her or his way; does not grasp teamwork
- not organized
- does not ask questions when he or she is not in the know
- not a good worker
- deceptive, not honest
- incompetent

Positive Attributes

- able to place herself or himself under the disciplines of teamwork
- respects authority

- cares for the customer's needs
- diligent at completing many tasks on an ongoing basis
- has common sense
- good communicator
- no guard rails for job performance (trait of an excellent performer)
- asks questions when he or she is not in the know
- knowledgeable of construction specifications and construction
- hungry to learn and has the capability to apply knowledge
- works overtime when conditions call for it
- not bashful
- relates well with customers
- works hard
- tough when she or he needs to be
- has staying power through difficult stretches

I know it may be hard to discern the true attributes of a person during an interview and due diligence process. You will have the candidate's cover letter and resume that were sent in response to the ad for the position, phone calls with the candidate, the interview process, perhaps a psychological test, and drug testing to review. I recommend that others be included in the interview process. Taking your time with this process will help ensure that the person selected has positive attributes in addition to his or her qualified work experience. If you end up with a person who possesses negative attributes, then it is going to be very hard to work with her or him. My experience is that people who have negative attributes are very unlikely to change their nature.

You are in the maintenance war with your staff. You and your staff live in a corporate fish bowl. Everyone will see the vendors coming and the work being done. If it is not done right, the complaints will come from many sides. It is easy to fail at this task. If you do, you will either quit or be fired. The heat will be immense. There are many moving parts, and any one of them can shipwreck everyone's efforts. Having a staff of people who care for what they do, are committed to following through with good service and vendor oversight, and deliver completed projects that satisfy their customers makes your job enjoyable and rewarding. I would do anything to help my facilities maintenance team. They put their full efforts on the line every day. How could I do any less?

Hopefully, you have a good staff of FMPMs. You then have a fighting chance to be highly successful meeting the maintenance needs of your company.

G. Vendors

In my facilities maintenance career, we desired to select capable and respected vendors to perform the maintenance required for the building components. We first selected three or more building component-specific companies to bid either a portion or all of our annual building component maintenance activity. For example, in my last position, I interviewed twelve HVAC companies to select one that we would give a contract for all our HVAC activity.

The desired attributes of a vendor closely mirror the comments made above for staff people. It was also very painful to find out that a vendor's person working with us exhibited many of the negative attributes listed above. When this happens, we first ask the vendor management to remove the person(s) working with us. If they didn't agree with our assessment, we would give it a second chance with their oversight of the matter. If no improvements were made and the vendor was reluctant to make the change, we needed to say goodbye to that vendor.

The metrics we used for evaluating our vendors were cost, time, and quality. Cost was king. Certainly, trust and personalities played a major role in the relationship as well. I knew that I would have a productive interview with a vendor when the representative came to the meeting and said, "What is it that you need to get accomplished, and how can we help you?" On the other hand, I knew that I was not going to have a productive interview when the vendor started out the meeting with, "Here's who we are, how we do things, and how we will help you with your maintenance program."

Company A had never had a national HVAC maintenance program. It took two years to get operation's 100 percent commitment, interview twelve companies, and have a contract in place for this program. Eight years later, the national HVAC program was so proficient in life cycle predictive and preventative maintenance that we handled the summer of 2012 with minimal noise all across the country. (Noise is what occurs when our customers—the store managers—complain.)

We had national building component maintenance programs for roofing, parking lots, overhead doors, HVAC, signs, lighting, and building and property electrical needs. We also set up a network of general contractors to address those building components and property maintenance needs that were not handled by the seven building components mentioned above. In all, the facilities maintenance area had eight three-year contracts with two two-year extensions possible written into the documents. The construction area administered the selection of and contracting with our sign vendors.

We had eleven national or regional vendors that were all under contract and performed nearly 85 percent of all our facilities maintenance projects. We recommended a number of them to operations for use within their custodial maintenance needs. There were twenty-four approved vendors in our vendor directory. Our top eleven vendors were considered not merely as vendors, but rather as program management companies for the building components for which they performed our maintenance needs.

I viewed the maintenance team, the FMPMs, and our team of vendors that got our work completed each year as an iceberg. What top—and middle-level management and anyone else who looked at facilities maintenance saw was the real estate facilities maintenance staff. That is the iceberg above the water line. Below the water line is the bulk of the iceberg—the national and regional vendors. Some of them self-perform a portion of the work they administer. All other work is performed by their approved subcontractors. We, the facilities maintenance staff, and the vendors are a team. All entities have to perform properly in order for the team to be successful. They are our partners.

Let me apply more detail to the vendor metrics.

1. Cost
    a. Labor, material, and profit and overhead
    b. Approved unit codes/unit costs of each work item
    c. Quotes in conformance with contract terms
    d. Applicable specifications adhered to
    e. Quote includes sketch or plan of improvements as needed
    f. Industry competitive costs
    g. Warranties specified
2. Time
    a. Response to customer service call
    b. Time for technician to be at the store to start work
    c. Timely follow-ups with technicians to track project progress
    d. Time to complete the work and not leaving location until complete
3. Quality
    a. Communications with the RE FMPM and store manager
        1) Company coming to store and when it will be there
        2) Implementing the sign in/sign out sheet upon arrival
        3) Through the progress of the improvement
        4) Close out the project with the sign in/sign out sheet
    b. Work performance
        1) Quality of the work completed
        2) Project cleanup and proper disposal of refuse

Consider that a person has about 230 work days in a year. There is a lot of activity happening each and every day. Of course, I don't have to explain that to anyone who works in this field. We don't have time for noise. Noise occurs when a maintenance project goes wrong and there are complaints, starting with those of the store manager. Depending on the store manager and/or the gravity of the problem, the level of complaints accelerates higher up the management chain. They can go from the assistant district manager to the district manager to the controller to the operations VP to the president of the company to the VP of real estate and then to the director or manager of facilities maintenance. *Ouch!*

Noise resolution takes you away from your ongoing workload. Noise is not a good thing. However, when you hear it, all hands are needed on deck to determine what is wrong, how it happened, who is responsible, and how the responsible party is going to resolve the matter. The matter has to be resolved fast, and in most cases, there is no cost involved.

In order to manage the facilities maintenance activity, which sometimes seems like a runaway freight train going down the side of a hill, we instituted red meetings with our top eleven vendors. These meetings could occur monthly or weekly, depending on the activity and complexity of that building component. These scheduled phone conference meetings included our entire facilities maintenance staff and the whole vendor team that worked on our projects. A meeting would cover the status of difficult projects and address any known noise issues.

The HVAC program has the most touch points with our customers and can generate the most noise. For this reason, we started meeting weekly to have proper oversight of this program. Our side had five people on the call, while our HVAC vendor (the majority of the time) had nine. We had such incredible management of this building component that during the summer of 2012, the hottest on record in the United States, we had no more than two units down at any given time across the country. This program was running so much like a high-efficiency engine that these meetings lasted about fifteen minutes. They went that long because there were a few professional baseball team updates that had to be shared.

As part of these red meetings, the vendors supplied updated reports of their activity for our maintenance needs. These reports were by zone, by expense and capital, and by active and complete. They would show the store, work underway or completed, costs, date started, date completed (if done), and most recent follow-up statement on the progress of the project.

We did not have database capability in-house, so we required that the following vendors maintain a database of our activity with them. The contract stated that we owned this data and could request transmission of our data whenever we needed to. These databases were set up to track the work done, document repairs and replacements of building components by store, and set up projections for life cycle replacements of the building components. We had excellent databases for our HVAC, lighting, and electrical panels programs. We had good and developing databases for our roofing and parking lot building components. We had an Excel spreadsheet of our overhead door activity.

There were sixty people from all the eleven vendors that participated in these red meeting phone conferences. These sixty people coordinated the activity of their many in-house technicians (if applicable) and their approved subcontractors to get our maintenance projects completed. That's the large part of the iceberg beneath the water line. There were approximately two thousand different technicians or subcontractors who performed our maintenance on an annual basis. It is this team of sixty people that coordinated that effort. Like in a relay race, we handed the baton of performance to them. This is a major component of corporate facilities maintenance. The aspect of performance management will be addressed later in more detail.

Our major vendors were a main resource of expertise that we tapped into to better understand the details of the building components they managed for us. We also scheduled two learning and team-building meetings with vendors each year. These events took three days, including travel to their offices and back home. These were great times to download information about the building components they managed for us. We also got to know better the teams of people within their companies who worked on our projects. There were great meals and fun events that we did together. I have many friends from the group of vendors we utilized to perform our maintenance needs. We had a tight iceberg. We knew that we needed each other to work in unison to be at maximum effect in servicing our store managers and district staff.

H. God Is in the Details

Details are important. How is something to be done? What materials are to be used? We need the right details—all of them; properly designed, documented, communicated, and implemented, they guarantee interested parties the results they expect. Doing something without the proper details in place is a recipe for a surprise—most often, a disappointment.

Consider a few facts about God's creation:

- The earth travels around the equator at 1,000 miles per hour.
- The earth orbits the sun at 67,000 miles per hour.
- The solar system travels around the center of the Milky Way galaxy at 490,000 miles per hour.
- The Milky Way galaxy hurtles through space at 1,300,000 miles per hour.
- There are billions of galaxies.
- There are estimated to be four hundred billion stars in the universe.

The only way these facts exist is because God is in the details. He created the universe to function the way it does. We are traveling right now at unimaginable speeds within our universe. Thank God that He is in the details. His creation is in order and functions with precision.

We should perform our facilities maintenance duties with order and precision. We should also be focused on the details within our universe of facilities maintenance. Don't assume anything. We need to have the details for processes and construction or work them out with our vendors. We need to make sure that the vendor personnel we work with are in complete agreement, because they have to make sure this information gets to their internal technicians or their subcontractors.

A completed maintenance project needs to provide the results that we paid for, guaranteeing no customer complaints. Give yourself high probability for success with your maintenance projects, and focus on the details first. Get the details right before you begin the improvements.

I put an example of details for a major parking lot process in Appendix C. There are so many people involved and a business to keep in operation—all the moving parts of the construction phase—that a detailed process is needed to perform many of these types of projects annually without noise. There is also an example of details for a board-up process after a break-in. Look at all the participants involved in this simple project and the coordination needed to assure that the board-up is performed properly.

Details are extremely important. Don't take shortcuts. It's like getting ready for your day. You shower, perform hygiene tasks at the sink, and put on clean clothes that meet the requirements for your day's activities. You don't want to shortchange this process. It just wouldn't feel right. To be good at facilities maintenance services, a person needs to have a sixth sense that he or she can't discharge a project until everything is reviewed, known, and stated. This person leaves nothing to chance. Just like someone wouldn't feel right leaving his or her house in the morning without brushing teeth, only having one shoe on, and forgetting to put a belt on, he or she they can't give a project to a vendor, technician, or contractor without knowing that all the details have been covered.

I. You Can't Manage What You Don't See

Directors and managers of facilities maintenance manage budgets, spending, vendors, the facilities maintenance staff, data entry into the computer system, maintenance projects performance, invoicing, and reporting to middle—and top-level management. There are a lot of moving parts to manage, and you can't manage what you don't see. Let's look at the concerns of the director or manager of facilities maintenance, get a handle on what is to be managed, and know what information we need to be successful.

What makes up the empire of our facilities maintenance responsibilities? How many divisions of the company are there? How many stores are within each division? What percentage of the stores within each division is leased? What percentage of the stores within each division is owned? What is the average age of the stores within each division? What are the oldest stores within each division? How many stores are more than twenty years old within each division? What is the average square foot area of the store's footprint within each division? What is the total square foot area of the entire store usage (including all areas of multiple floors) within each division?

We need to get this data from many different sources. We need to be aggressive in tracking down this information. Check with the VP of real estate, the company controller, and the reports available for this information within the accounting and operations departments. Once you get access to the right reports, ask to be put on the distribution list of these reports for the future. By doing so, you will stay in the know about this ever-changing data.

To know custodial maintenance information, one must ask, What maintenance programs make up custodial maintenance? What is the annual budget for custodial maintenance? What is the annual spending of each of these maintenance programs? How does the custodial spending compare to budget? How are these maintenance programs managed? What is the annual cost per square foot of buildings for the company's custodial maintenance?

Most likely, you will find this data where I did—in the accounting department. Again, ask to be put on the future distribution list for updates on these reports.

Facilities maintenance information includes the following questions: What maintenance programs presently make up facilities maintenance? What is the annual budget for facilities maintenance? What type of facilities maintenance program does the company want? Does the company want to fix it when it breaks with little to no regard for the building component life cycles and deferred maintenance, create a predictive and preventative maintenance program that addresses all building components, or a combination of the two approaches? What maintenance programs improvements will you implement? How are these maintenance programs presently managed? How are you going to improve the management of these programs? What is the annual spending of each of these maintenance programs? How does the facilities maintenance spending compare to budget? What is the annual cost per square foot for facilities maintenance spending? What is the combined annual cost per square foot for the company's custodial and facilities maintenance programs?

This data is in your wheelhouse, so to speak. The real estate accounting function will be helpful. Your team will generate much of this data in the course of completing facilities maintenance projects. Get a handle on it so you see where you are and where you will take the facilities maintenance program.

For facilities maintenance staff performance information, ask, What are the active and closed project counts at the end of each month, on a monthly and year-to-date basis, for each of the FMPMs? Is the workload evenly assigned to each FMPM? Are any FMPMs not performing as they should? Does each FMPM properly enter the project tracking data into the computer system? Are the right decisions on how to address project management-type projects made by each FMPM? Do the FMPMs keep up with the agreed-to timing for processing invoices? Do the FMPMs communicate appropriately with our customers? Do any of the FMPMs have unresolved issues with a vendor?

Reports will have to be generated on the computer system to track a lot of this information. Don't assume anything. Have the data so that you can manage it. Some of this data will be apparent to you as you stay engaged in the day-to-day activities of your team.

For vendors' performance information, ask, Do vendors communicate properly with our customers? Do they submit quotes and/ or perform their work for us with pricing in accordance with the contract? Is the timing of their work within agreed-to standards? Is the quality of their work proper? Is the reporting of their work activity kept up-to-date? Do they properly database their work (if required)? Do they attend our red meetings prepared to discuss their activity? Are the vendor's invoices submitted soon after the completion of their work?

The data for these concerns will be apparent as you work with and get feedback from your FMPMs on their interactions with the vendors. Feedback from the store managers is solicited from the FMPMs on completion of projects in many cases. Ask them to share disappointments the customers have with facilities maintenance. The red meetings are a great resource to keep abreast of the day-to-day activity of the vendors. Their monthly reporting also lets you know if they are diligently keeping the status of projects up-to-date.

To learn accounting information, ask, What is the budget for each facilities maintenance program? What is the spending for each program at the end of each month on a year-to-date basis? What directions need to be given to either speed up or slow down the spending of each program to be on target at the year's end?

The budget becomes known as the director or manager of facilities maintenance works with the VP of real estate and the accounting personnel to present the proposed annual budget to top-level management. Once approved, this sets the spending caps for each facilities maintenance program. The FMPMs enter the project tracking for their projects, including money spent and money approved to be spent. A computer report is prepared to show the total spending information on a monthly year-to-date basis. This data is tracked against the annual budgets. We can then provide estimated spending projections for the remainder of the calendar year and indicate whether we will hit the budget.

When reporting to middle and top levels of management, ask what information they want to see on a monthly basis. The accounting information mentioned above is on top of their list. Information on the timing of the projects is beneficial. What is the volume of projects for each building component, and what percentage of these projects was performed within timing standards?

There is a lot to see so we can properly manage what the company pays us to do. If you don't have the data from reports, feedback, or firsthand knowledge of any of the areas mentioned above, then you have a management blind spot in that area(s). You can't manage what you can't see.

J.   Unit Code/Unit Cost

There are many restaurants or stores in a company's portfolio of locations—hundreds, sometimes thousands. Many of the building components are the same or similar throughout the chain of restaurants or stores. We need to repair or replace these building components many times throughout the year. If we bid out the building components replacement costs to qualified manufacturers, vendors, and contractors and select the low bidders, then we can continue to award maintenance projects to these companies on an ongoing basis. Why do we have to repetitively bid out every building component repair or replacement project?

The advantages of having one approved vendor for each building component are competitive prices being used in all cases, uniformity of project performance throughout stores, and contracts with these companies that cover all aspects of our working relationship (including pricing, insurance, warranties, invoicing, working requirements, legal requirements, and the ability to proceed quickly with projects as they arise).

In my last position, the company approved real estate facilities maintenance having contracts with manufacturers, vendors, and contractors, allowing them to proceed with maintenance work based on a unit code/unit cost basis with a single bid up to $10,000. Unit codes are the individual construction line items of a project. For example, if we replace ten overhead doors with each door costing $2,800, then bids are not needed. Even though the project cost is $28,000, the unit cost (one door) is $2,800. With the unit cost being less than $10,000, one bid is needed.

The roofing building component was managed by one roofing manufacturer. It had approved roofing contractors across the country. The company had a team of people who managed our reroofing projects. They got three approved roofing contractors to bid each project. Roofing repairs were generally less than $10,000; therefore, they were able to get a roofing contractor in the area of the store and have the contractor address the leak issue quickly.

The parking lot component was managed by one paving company. It operated much like the roofing building component company.

The HVAC building component was managed by one HVAC/facilities maintenance company. Because our HVAC units were primarily five—to 7.5-ton units and the cost per unit was under $10,000, we didn't have to get bids. The HVAC, heater, and exhaust fan servicing was set up so the store managers could contact the vendor directly. The service work could be done directly if the cost was $1,499 or less. The HVAC vendor would coordinate over two thousand of these projects on an annual basis. I would receive bulk invoicing for these projects and approve them for our accounting area to process for payment. The FMPMs were not involved with these projects for the most part.

The overhead door building component was managed by one overhead manufacturing company. With the cost of each door always being less than $10,000, we never had to get bids for overhead door replacements.

Signage was contracted out to three companies through our construction department. These contracts required each sign company to price out each type of sign and repairs to signs. In this way, we never had to get bids for maintenance projects.

Electrical building component issues were managed by one electrical and facilities maintenance company. We had a program to inspect every electrical panel, a program to inspect every store's electrical outlets, and another program to address electrical service calls. The unit cost for electrical panels and service issues did not go over $10,000; therefore, we didn't have to procure bids.

Lighting building component issues were managed by one service company. Each unit cost of these improvements was nowhere near $10,000; therefore, bids were not required.

General contracting issues often went over $10,000 with multiple line items of improvements; therefore, bids were required. However, if a project was to paint the outside of a store and the cost of the project was $12,000 but the cost per square foot for prep and paint was in agreement with our cost standards, we could award this project based on unit code/unit cost guidelines.

This spending management approach allows the real estate facilities maintenance team to respond quickly to address the maintenance needs of our stores. Consider that the stores call us in most cases in an emergency nature—the roof is leaking, the parking lot has a pothole, the electrical panel is buzzing, etc. We can now move quickly to address these maintenance needs and are not held back trying to get three bids. We are also reusing our approved vendors or contractors to do these projects. They become very proficient with these projects. This saves the FMPMs time, as they do not have to educate or train technicians or subcontractors the specifications and processes that we want applied.

This has also allowed us to set up programs in which the store can call the vendor directly, and the vendor can go to the store and make the immediate repair up to $1,499 (approved not to exceed cost).

Response time is maximized under this NTE program. Work quality is maximized, because the approved vendors have dedicated personnel working on our maintenance needs. They are familiar with our projects, processes, people, and prices. They manage the many technicians and subcontractors needed to get the maintenance work performed. There is uniformity in materials used and the specifications for the projects. In this way, we partner with the store managers to better serve our retail customers—the boss! A unit codes form is shown in Appendix E.

K. Life Cycle of Building Components

From my thirty years of facilities maintenance management experience, the figures below show the life cycle years for the building components that I am familiar with. It is very important to know these figures or what the specific life cycle years are for the building components you are responsible for. In doing so, you are better able to know when to repair or replace a building component and estimate your annual capital spending for building component replacements.

I always asked, "How many years did that shop heater last?" when someone told me that she or he was replacing some in a store. It was amazing how often I heard the FMPM tell me, "Eighteen years." Yes, some lasted seventeen years, and some lasted nineteen years, but the majority lasted eighteen years. I knew that the life cycle for shop heaters was eighteen years. I recently read a professional HVAC document that referenced life cycles of equipment. What life cycle do you think it listed for shop heaters? Eighteen years!

Our experience over the years with the life cycles of building components is a reliable source of information. Below is the list of life cycles for the most common building components that we had to deal with over my last thirty years of facilities maintenance management.

Building Component   **Years**

Roofing

Placing a roof membrane over an existing roof membrane	10
Single-ply roofing membrane system—minimal thickness	16
Modified bitumen roofing membrane system	16
Cap sheet BUR roofing system	16
Single-ply roofing membrane system (60 mil fully adhered)	20
Metal roofing (before repairs, coating, or roof over)	24-28

HVAC

Shop area heaters	18
Package HVAC units	15

Electrical

Lighting—T-8 fluorescent lamps (Company A usage)	5
Lighting—electronic ballasts	10
Electrical Panels	40

Plumbing

Municipal utilities

Sanitary sewers—VCT, cast iron	50
Sanitary sewers—PVC	50+
Storm sewers—concrete	50
Water main—cast iron	50
Water main—ductile iron, PVC	50+

Doors

Overhead doors	20
Front entrance and metal man doors	25

Signage

Flex face signs	12
Rigid face signs	15
Ballasts	10
LEDs	10

Concrete

Sidewalks, curbs, steps/landings, pads, parking lots	20+

Asphalt

Fill potholes	0.5-1
Crack filling, seal, and stripe	3
Full depth plus patching	5
Two-inch mill and overlay	12
Complete asphalt removal and proper thickness replacement (with proper maintenance)	20

Exterior

Painting CMU walls	5-8

The building components should be inspected when replacement is anticipated. If additional years can be realized from the existing building component, they can get minimal repairs and move the replacement out a set number of years.

L. Repair/Replacement Guidelines

It is incredible how people will continually repair a building component or piece of equipment well beyond its useful life. I believe that they believe they are saving money. Very rarely is that the case. What information can we use to better determine when we should repair or replace something? As an engineer, I was looking for a graph. After more than twenty years in the facilities maintenance workplace, I had a lot of firsthand experience. I believed that there was a relationship between the repair or replacement decision and the plotting of the life cycle and replacement cost of the building component or piece of equipment. The graph that I developed is as follows:

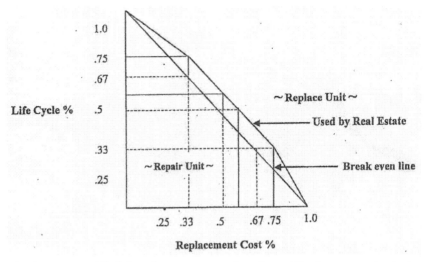

Equipment and Building Components—Repair and Replacement Analysis
Evaluating Life Cycle and Replacement Cost Data

The low-cost option *for today* is many times the wrong basis for determining whether to repair a piece of equipment or building component. Each time a repair or replacement decision needs to be made, the decision-maker should take into account the typical life cycle of the item under consideration, the age of the item, the typical replacement cost, and the repair cost. With this data available, a decision can be made that optimizes the spending decision—a decision based on the life cycle of the item, not the low-cost option *for today.*

For example, a fifteen-year-old overhead door needs to have a metal panel replaced, because it has been damaged, and there is a section of window that needs to be replaced, because it is cracked. The cost to make the repairs is $1,000. The life cycle of overhead doors is twenty years. The cost to replace the overhead door is $2,500.

Draw a horizontal line from the 75 percent mark of the item's life cycle and a vertical line from the 40 percent mark of replacement cost. These lines intersect above the dividing line or repair and replace; therefore, we should replace the overhead door.

The overhead door might last another five years with the repairs. Therefore, that is an annual cost of improvement of $1,000/five years = $200/year. Consider the replacement of the door—an annual cost of $2,500/twenty years = $125/year. So if the overhead door did last another five years and we replaced it, we lost $375 over that five-year period on a comparative annual amortized cost analysis. Other factors to consider if we did the repair:

- This door would have a new manufactured white panel, and all the other doors and the one or two panels of the same door have dirty, fifteen-year-old, dinged-up panels. How does this look from the street? Not good.
- The fifteen-year-old door has double-strength glass sections. The new glass replacement section is safety-tempered glass. Considering the cost analysis and the other factors, it makes sense to replace this door. It would be good to inspect the other nine doors at this location and determine their condition, because it might make sense to replace more than one door. In the repair or replace decision, we have the life cycle in years of the building component, the cost to install a new building component, determine the cost to repair the building component for somewhere from one to five years and the Repair or Replace Analysis Chart. We need to also know the following information;
- If leased, who has responsibility of the building component repair and replacement?
- If owned, are there plans to close or relocate this store?
- What is the condition of the building component? Review photos.
- What is the history of repairs done to this building component?
- Is there a safety or operational issue with the building component?
- What is the cost of the replacement amortized over the life cycle of the building component? We will call this annual cost x.
- What are the years required for the repair cost to be cost-efficient? Divide the repair cost by the amortized annual cost

of the replacement *(x)*. This will provide the number of years that the repairs will need to last, and we can then decide if the repair is cost-effective. We will need to make an evaluation if the building component is expected to last that many more years with the proposed repair.

Example of this repair or replacement cost justification: A twenty-one-year-old HVAC unit needs a new compressor. This is an owned store that we will be at for a long time. The 7.5-ton HVAC unit replacement cost is $11,000. The life cycle for a new HVAC unit is fifteen years. The new compressor cost is $3,000.

$11,000/fifteen years = $733.33 amortized per year cost = *x*. $3,000/$733.33 amortized per year replacement cost = 4.09 years.

Will a twenty-one-year-old HVAC unit with a new compressor last 4.09 more years? If the unit fails after one year with the repair made, we lost $3,000—$733.33 = $2,266.67.

Given this scenario, the best decision is to replace the unit. An old unit will typically die, because the rest of the parts can't keep up with the new compressor. Consider also the energy efficiency of the new unit versus the old unit.

Too many times, people who don't have a full knowledge of the repair or replacement issues will default to the low-cost fix option. Safety issues arise, energy options are ignored, and repair costs will be lost, because the building component or piece of equipment will not last long enough to be cost-effective.

My car needed servicing. I set up an appointment with the local store that I frequented. Upon arriving at the store, I found the store manager upset. I asked him what the matter was. He said that his tire changer was not working properly, so he took it apart to see if he could fix it, but he couldn't. So he called his assistant district manager and asked him to approve a new tire changer. His boss said, "No, call the dealer, and get it repaired." He was very upset, because he knew this was a waste of time, and he needed this piece of equipment.

The dealer came out, looked at the part causing the problem, and told the store manager, "This unit is so old, and we don't make that part anymore." He then was given approval for the new unit.

The store manager explained to me that the tire changer was so old that it needed a lot of repairs and was dangerous to use. This story just reinforces the mindset of so many—to just keep fixing things and spend minimal funds to address every situation. This approach wastes money, fosters deferred maintenance, puts off the repair or replacement analysis, and could cause a safety issue.

M. Reporting

Monthly

1. Projects and Spending Tracking Report
   This report lists the budget sub-programs and has the following data: show by region or zone the capital and expense activity—active projects and dollar amount and completed projects and dollar amount—and then show the total committed dollars for capital and expense. Also show the capital and expense budgets and the plus/minus of the committed dollars to the budget. The average days to complete the projects are shown to the right of the complete dollars column. Each budget sub-program will have a total line showing all the information stated above. At the Company A, our tracked budget sub-programs were: HVAC, roofs, parking lots, overhead doors, signs, lighting, electrical panels, electrical wiring and outlets, special projects, general maintenance, and store expense (the project totals and dollars managed that were included in the operations' custodial maintenance budget). This report will provide the total number of projects and dollars committed that the facilities maintenance team is or has been involved with on a year-to-date (YTD) basis. This report will provide you the picture of the activity of all the building components and the other general budget sub-programs. See an example of this form on Appendix F.

2. Spending Summary and Year-End (YE) Estimated Total Spending for Capital and Expense (separate reports)
   This report will list down the side the capital budget sub-

programs, and on a separate report, the expense budget sub-programs. Across the top of the report, there will be the following column headers: actual spent (completed projects spending), pending (active projects with company approval to proceed with either a purchase order or approved not to succeed—committed dollars), maybe to 12/31 (estimated spending from this point in the year to the end of the year), YE estimated total (the dollar total projected to be spent), budget (the sub-program budget), and B/W (the amount under budget or over budget). Then the bottom of the report will show the total capital estimated spending, the budget, and the estimated better or worse to the budget. These two reports—capital and expense—are good spending dashboard reports to show where you are at during the year and where you intend to end up at the end of the year. See Appendices G and H for example forms for capital and expense.

3. Projects Timing Performance Report
   You should have predetermined timing performance standards for each building component. There would be a number of acceptable days to perform repairs and another number of acceptable days to perform a replacement for each building component. Within this programming would be the recommended follow-ups for emergency, repair and replacement projects for each building component. The follow-up process is the hammer that drives the project to a proper completion. The computer system should determine the actual days it took to complete each project by subtracting the start date from the completed date. The computer should also determine the number of projects, per building component, that were completed within the timing standards and the number that were completed over the timing standards. The results of this data are on the projects timing performance report. See Appendix I for a sample form. I would tell management that our goal was to have 80 percent of our projects completed within the project's timing performance

standards. The reason the number was not 100 percent was because there are twenty-two reasons outside our control that could delay the project. If a project was late, we would list one of the twenty-two reasons. These twenty-two reasons are approval by management to proceed, approval by the lease transactions manager, approval by operations, bids (securing three), bids (inability to get three), complexity of issue, delay in construction start, environmental issues, holiday delays, mall owner issue, landlord issue, lease renegotiations, legal issue, material ordering or delivery, multiple trades on project, permitting, punch out items remaining, store scheduling difficulties to perform the work, problems with the subcontractor, vendor performance, weather, and winter (would shut down outside projects in snow climate regions).

Annually

1. YE and Year Beginning reports

   In the beginning of the new year, run all your YE reports for the completed year, and keep these reports on file. These will enable you to create a history report of the facilities maintenance program over time. The years go by quickly, and there should be a report that shows the results by year over time. Now run the beginning year report. This report will have no completed project within the last year shown on this report. It will only show those carryover projects—either started and not completed or never started and still intend for completion.

2. Predictive Spending Analysis to Assist with Budget Preparation

   Determine the budget sub-programs anticipated capital spending. For example, let's look at roofing:

   (# of stores at which we are responsible for replacement) x (average sq. ft. area of each roof) x (Est. $/sq. ft.) / (twenty-year roof life cycle) = estimated dollars/year

Also, (# of stores at which we are responsible for replacement) / (twenty-year life of stores) = # of reroof projects

This analysis is only germane if the average age of your locations is twenty years or more. If you have a newer chain of locations, track the number of reroof stores by those that are actually twenty years or older. This analysis would then be performed for all your large building component budget sub-programs. The general maintenance and special projects capital budgets will just have prior history figures used for the budget analysis. Compare your building component life cycle annual cost estimates with the prior year's budget and actual spending. Add up your estimated budget sub-programs figures, get a total for capital, divide your capital total by the total square foot area of all the stores, and determine your cost per square foot capital budget request for facilities maintenance. The expense process will utilize the previous year's budget figures and the annual spending of the current year to put forth each line item figure. Now add these figures together, divide by the total square foot area of all the stores, and determine your cost per square foot expense budget request for facilities maintenance. Then adding the capital and expense cost per square foot figures together will give you your total cost per square foot facilities maintenance budget request.

3. YE Facilities Maintenance Summary Spending Report
List all of your budget sub-programs down the left side of the page. Across the top of the page will be a capital column, an expense column, and a total column. Fill in the actual spending totals for the end of the year. At the bottom, you will have your total spending for capital and expense and the total. The total dollar amount divided by the total square footage of all the stores determines your facilities maintenance cost per square foot for the year. Add the YE custodial cost per square foot to the facilities maintenance YE cost per square foot. This provides the annual total maintenance square foot cost for the company.

N. "Fix It When It Breaks" Maintenance Program

This approach to facilities maintenance gives little to no regard for the life cycle of the building components and equipment or for deferred maintenance. As discussed in the repair/replacement guidelines paragraph above, the decision-makers will err on the side of the apparent low-cost option and make repairs instead of replacing the building component or equipment when it is at or beyond life cycle. Usually, there is no ongoing maintenance to meet or extend the life cycle of the building components or equipment. When there is an emergency situation, maintenance is done.

The following excerpt is from an article entitled "Delivering Effective Facility Management," published in the Professional Retail Store Maintenance magazine (in two parts) in their December 2001/January 2002 and February 2002 issues. I wrote this article and have retyped it in Appendix L.

> [5]How important is the maintenance of your facilities to your customers? For most customers, it is the top priority. Many practices in place at multi-site corporations fail to give facility maintenance and repair this same priority or importance. While marketing and sales efforts are increasingly more customer centric, facilities practices and programs have not kept pace. Many practices relegate facility maintenance to an afterthought rather than view it as an important part of encouraging and sustaining customer loyalty.

The lack of needed ongoing maintenance and improper maintenance when the building components or equipment are near or beyond their life cycle are the reasons that this approach to facilities maintenance can only provide a level of facilities maintenance from an *F* to a *C*. There are two developments within this maintenance program that allow it to be a *C* rather than an *F*. The first is if guidelines are put in place to activate maintenance action. These guidelines

---

[5]   Al Tierney, "Delivering Effective Facility Management," *Professional Retail Store Maintenance,* December 2001/January 2002 and February 2002, 38, 28.

have the definition of "must do," "should do," and "would like to do" maintenance projects.

Must Do

1. Repair or replace building components as needed so long-term performance of the building is not affected.
2. Repair or replace property and building components that are not functioning safely.
3. Specify maintenance work required as part of a lease renewal.
4. Repair building issues that affect store operations.

Should Do

1. Repair or replace property and building components that function poorly.

Would Like to Do

1. Repair or replace property and building components that affect the property's appearance.
2. Perform non-essential property and building new installations and improvements.

Budget constraints will many times dictate that only "must do" projects can be performed by direction of the director or manager of facilities maintenance. "should do" and "would like to do" projects can be performed if directed by top and middle management.

The second development that raises the grade of the level of maintenance service is the addition of a refresh or reimage program. These programs can vary from major remodeling and maintenance attention to improving the appearance with minimal expenditures. These programs can vary from a five-year program to a ten-year program. The closer to five years and the greater the improvements, the higher the level of maintenance service grade could be.

This approach to facilities maintenance, if utilized for many years, allows deferred maintenance to build up. There will come a moment in time when the building components will begin to fail. Exterior walls will begin to lose brick faces, block walls will crack, roof decks will rust out, parking lots will become severely potholed, electrical panels will become unsafe, exterior signs won't function properly, showroom floor tiles will become loose, interior walls will become dirty, some lighting lamps will burn out, doors will not close properly, property trees will die, and dumpsters will be in disrepair. When this happens, the expectations of low square foot maintenance costs have vanished. Now six figures and up are most likely needed to bring the store back into company desired use.

O. Predictive and Preventative Maintenance Program

It is here that I must share with you part of my facilities maintenance story. I was with Company B as its manager of facilities maintenance. We had over 350 branches nationwide. I had two facilities maintenance project managers. The average age of the branches was about twenty years. I had been in my position for nearly ten years.

The operations service manager met with me and stated that the company wanted a facilities maintenance program where the maintenance items were known upfront and the budget could be established over the years with little to no fluctuation. My response was, "How can that be done?"

His response was, "I don't know, but you will do it!" That meeting changed my facilities maintenance career forever. No longer did we fix things when they broke. My facilities maintenance career elevated into the predictive and preventative mode.

The two facilities maintenance project managers and I went into a whiteboard room. All the walls were whiteboards, from the floor to the ceiling. We set out to give the company what it wanted. First, we listed all the repetitive maintenance issues we did day in and day out for the branches. I remember this as if it were yesterday. There were thirty-two issues listed: roof leaks, parking lot patching, lighting, HVAC, etc. We then listed the period of years that the repairs or replacements generally lasted. It was then that the wall started to talk to us. Sixteen of the items were general maintenance, and the other sixteen were of a remodel nature. The maintenance items were mostly within a four-year life cycle.

We changed some that were three to four and some that were five to four. The remodel items were mostly within an eight-year life cycle. Again, we had to change a few to line up all items with an eight-year life. We then decided to list those maintenance and remodel items that would typically be present for a four-, eight-, twelve-, sixteen-, and twenty-year-old store. We were going to walk through time, so to speak, and predetermine the typical maintenance and remodel issues that existed at each four-year interval of a store's life for up to twenty years. We could stop at twenty years, because the life cycles of all the building components are twenty years or fewer, and if you repair and replace (as needed), the twenty-year-old store should not look too different from a new store with the same layout. See the life cycle maintenance and repair scheduled tasks that we developed in Appendix J.

We put estimated costs to each line item, thereby determining if the item was capital or expense. We were then able to have an estimated capital and expense cost for each four-years maintenance list of anticipated maintenance improvements. The three of us were responsible for 100 or more branches. We went through each store and determined (the best we could) what year the store was at, considering its age, and what repairs and replacements had been done thus far. Starting out, we were probably 80 percent accurate with our year selections for each store, but considering that we were going to evaluate the maintenance needs for every store once every four years, we would be 100 percent exact in four years.

It was amazing how this predictive and preventative maintenance program changed the phone calls we received from the store managers once they were aware of how their maintenance needs were going to be met. Rather than emergency phone calls being the order of the day, they would call with one question: "When is my store up for the four-year maintenance inspection?"

See the real estate maintenance and repair schedule definition in Appendix K. This program was very regulated. The seventy-five or so stores on the four-year maintenance schedule for a given year would be inspected in the fall before the budget year to determine the actual list of maintenance work required. Then quotes for the work would be submitted by the end of the year. The three of us would handle twenty-five or so stores. We would inspect the eight— and sixteen-year stores with the general contractors. We would have general contractors inspect alone or with us the four-, twelve-, and twenty-year stores. The three of us would know what reroofs, parking lot replacements, HVAC replacements, overhead door replacements, and all other replacements were on our schedule for next year. We would get our national building component vendors to bid out this work and have the work approved by early spring. We wanted to be first on the vendors work scope for the year. We also wanted our projects done by the end of September. This was truly a grade-A level of maintenance service program.

About four years after I left this company, I had a conversation with one of the construction project managers of that company. He told me that they were selling a handful of stores in a certain city and relocating them to where there was a greater concentration of customers. He said that the stores sold quickly and for more than the area comps because they were so well-maintained.

The predictive and preventative maintenance program allows the Real Estate Facilities Maintenance area to take the building maintenance concerns off the backs of operations and allow them to focus on the business—meeting the customer's needs, providing a positive experience every time, and being profitable. This ensures that safety issues are negated, the building components operate as intended, the appearance of the property and building are competitive, the morale of the teammates who work at the store is higher, and the store is given the greatest opportunity for success that the building components can provide. This type of maintenance program will have a typical store maintenance cost about double that of an F "fix it when it breaks" store maintenance cost.

However, if your chain of stores has an average age of twenty-five or more years, the deferred maintenance will come crashing down on the perceived "fix it when it breaks" maintenance program. These stores that are older than twenty-five years will literally begin falling apart, and major funds are needed to bring the store back to usefulness. These costs could approximate twenty times the regular square foot maintenance cost of a store. Even though the perceived square foot cost per store of the "fix it when it breaks" facilities maintenance program is one half that of the predictive and preventive facilities maintenance program, the actual annual cost difference savings for all stores will only be about 12 percent less. The reason for the closeness of the costs is the large costs they will experience to address the deferred maintenance on stores that are twenty-five years old and older.

Consider also if that much deferred maintenance still exists, the level of maintenance service is low, and the boss and our teammates are negatively impacted with the subpar maintenance and operation of the stores. Given the negative effects, is there really a 12 percent savings of maintenance costs with the "fix it when it breaks" option? No, there isn't. Consider the legal issues with accidents with our teammates and customers. Consider the loss of business due to the lack of proper maintenance as perceived by our customers. Plus, what type of brand image do we portray to our customers and employees?

I challenge anyone in top—and middle-level management positions to evaluate the whole picture of these two types of maintenance programs. When everything is put on the scales of evaluation, you will not applaud the "fix it when it breaks" program.

The predictive and preventative maintenance program at Company B was running so smoothly that I left to promote the Program to other companies. About a year later, the attacks of September 11 happened, and work was hard to come by. Within another year, I joined Company A. The company wanted someone to come in and start a predictive and preventative maintenance program. This was a great opportunity to build a top-notch facilities maintenance program with all the techniques that I had learned from Company B.

It took five years to develop the building component life cycle capital replacement and expense repairs programs. We instituted a ten-year maintenance cycle to complement the existing ten-year reimage cycle. In this way, every store was going to be inspected once every five years, because the two programs were offset by five years. The store inspections of each of these programs would pick up the maintenance needs that were outside the building component programs. The program went well the first year we had it established and budgeted. However, the next year, the economy started to slide in a negative direction, and the company decided to reduce the budget of its maintenance program. So in my last four years of being the director of facilities maintenance, I managed a combination of a "fix it when it breaks" and predictive and preventative facilities maintenance program.

P. Combination of "Fix It When It Breaks" and Predictive and Preventative Programs

Let's review the possible toolsets, so to speak, for each of the two maintenance programs we have just described.

Fix It When It Breaks

1. Establish "must do," "should do," and "would like to do" guidelines.
2. Establish a refresh, remodel, or reimage program—anywhere from a five- to ten-year cycle.
3. Field emergency calls from the stores.

Predictive and Preventative

1. Create building components and equipment life cycle databases.
2. Gather a history of repairs and replacements of building components for each store.
3. Create a refresh, remodel, or reimage program—anywhere from a five- to ten-year cycle.
4. Create a maintenance cycle in concert with the ten-year cycle so every store is addressed every five years or the maintenance concerns are included in the five-year refresh, remodel, or reimage program.
5. Perform life cycle inspection and replacement if necessary for the following building components: roofs, parking lots, HVAC units, and overhead doors. If no replacement is needed,

then perform repairs to extend usefulness of the building component from one to five years.

6. Establish a sign maintenance program.
7. Create an electrical panels and systems maintenance program.
8. Establish a lighting maintenance program.
9. Create a budget to handle building components that don't have their own budgets.

Top- and middle-level management can decide to take some components of the predictive and preventative maintenance program out to reduce the facilities maintenance budget. They do not give any credence to the deferred maintenance issue. Deferred maintenance is like a cancer that is allowed to grow. There will come a time when the building will be in such a state of disrepair that the upfront savings will all but be taken back, because there will be a point of payback. Those building components that were allowed to reach dysfunction will have to be replaced.

People in top- and middle-management positions will change, and they will bring their preconceived thoughts on facilities maintenance services and costs with them. They provide the management direction for the company's facilities maintenance program. The discussion of what facilities maintenance program is to be in place will always be in play.

The first toolset to go from the predictive and preventative maintenance program is the maintenance cycle that compliments the refresh, remodel, or reimage programs. The next piece of the program to go is part of (or all of) the life cycle building component replacements. The grade of the level of maintenance service slides from an *A* to a *C* quickly. The *why* of facilities maintenance is compromised for the supposed quick budget savings that, as we have stated above, do not really exist in the long run. We need to realize that for every action, there are consequences. Are the consequences of inferior facilities maintenance understood? There are a lot of dynamics affected—the customer's (the boss) perspective of our store, store's employees' morale, safety of the building components and equipment, and most likely, sales.

Q. Facilities Maintenance—Necessary Evil or Good?

This question is really addressed to top- and middle-level management. If a person thinks facilities maintenance is a necessary evil, then she or he is prone to apply minimal effort and funds to it, thereby taking a short-sighted view and not looking at the long-term effects of the lack of maintenance. These people have a lot on their minds and do not allow themselves to fully understand the dynamics of facilities maintenance. If upper management sees facilities maintenance as a necessary evil, then they focus primarily on the budget issues. This thinking leads them to reduce the facilities maintenance budget and correspondingly the facilities maintenance efforts. The bottom line is that they just don't have time to understand it, and believe facilities maintenance spending can be reduced. They say, "It affects our bonus, so let's cut these costs."

It is very apparent that I see facilities maintenance as a necessary good. I have been a weekend cross-trainer bike rider for years. About a year and a half ago, I took notice of bike riders on road bikes and in fancy outfits. I reasoned that I'm not getting any younger and that I owe it to myself to check out road bikes, experience the speed, and wear the fancy outfits. So I bought a road bike in November of 2011. I had to start going to spin classes to get in better shape and to help me get used to the lock-in-pedal shoes.

In August of last year, a couple guys in the spin class asked if I wanted to join their thirty-mile bike ride the upcoming Saturday. I had the bike, the clothes, had attended the spin classes, and had been on a couple thirty-mile rides with a friend, so I joined them. That morning, there were twenty-two riders. At 8:30 a.m., we took off and went through a couple of subdivisions two-by-two as we headed to the country roads. Through the subdivisions, I did fine. I began to think, *Look at me; I'm a road biker.*

I was brought to reality pretty quick. We crossed the major road and were on country roads that had hills. As we hit the hills, I didn't see the other twenty riders. Thankfully, the leader came back and explained to me that no one is left behind and that he would stay with me—poor guy. He mercifully suggested that we not take one section of the thirty-mile ride that was very hilly. "Thank you," I said.

I did finish about twenty-five miles and arrived back at the starting point with the other riders. That bike ride was the hardest I ever did in my life. However, it was the best bike ride that I ever did, because it motivated me. It helped me to see more clearly a few things. I was overweight and had taken rides with people who didn't go that fast. For the first time in my life, I saw eating right as a necessary good! If I lost weight, I would feel better and have a better chance to ride a road bike like those people did that Saturday morning. Now I am much more conscious about eating properly. I see the benefits to it, and the more I do it, the better I feel. I've now lost nearly twenty pounds, and I want to lose more. I am in spin classes three times a week. I'm looking forward to trying that ride again.

Facilities maintenance is like eating right—it is a necessary good. Look at all the positive aspects of a predictive and preventative maintenance program:

- We address the safety and security needs of our teammates and customers.
- We maximize the operational effectiveness of the use or purpose of the building components and equipment.
- We present a property and building appearance that is as good as or better than those of our competitors.
- The company brand is maintained across the breadth of its stores, regardless of the stores' ages.
- We maintain the company assets, enabling them to be used for many years.
- We provide a building envelop that is waterproofed.
- We provide a working environment that promotes positive morale.
- We support the store manager in her or his efforts to provide a positive experience for the customers.
- We reduce the chance of maintenance emergencies that could impact the store's business.
- We reduce the chance of lawsuits that arise from accidents at our stores due to poorly-maintained building components or equipment.

- We provide the store manager with the greatest opportunity of success with a properly maintained property and store. Marketing drives the customers to the stores, and facilities maintenance gives a greater likelihood that they will come back.
- There is little to no deferred maintenance.

When someone truly realizes the benefits and results of a predictive and preventative maintenance program, how could he or she want to wipe them away with the stroke of a budget cut? Has this person quantified the value of adding the proper maintenance program?

VI

Facilities Maintenance Project Managers

These people carry out the day-to-day facilities maintenance management applications. They will need to own a bunch of those positive attitudes stated earlier in Facilities Maintenance Staffing. This job will wear you down otherwise. If a FMPM has some of the negative attributes, he or she will function like a car with three tires low on air and one flat. There will be friction with everyone—the customer, the vendors, and the director or manager of facilities maintenance. It will be hard for everyone in this person's wake. It is best if a change is made to get all FMPMs working as a team. Most likely, the staff is lean, and there is no room to carry a non-performer or live with this frustration.

A. Project Management

I looked up the term *project management,* and I was sent to Wikipedia. There was a thirteen-page response. The following are portions of this response:

[6]"As a discipline, project management developed from several fields of application including civil construction, engineering, and heavy defense activity. Two forefathers of project management are Henry Gantt, called the father of planning and control techniques, who is famous for his use of the Gantt chart as a project management

tool, and Henri Fayol for his creation of the five management functions that form the foundation of the body of knowledge associated with project and program management. The 1950s marked the beginning of the modern project management era when core engineering fields come together to work as one. At the same time, as project-scheduling models were being developed, technology for project cost estimating, cost management, and engineering economics was evolving, with pioneering work by Hans Lang and others."

"Project Management,"
Wikipedia, accessed January 7, 2013.
http://www.wikipedia.com/project management.

[7]"A traditional phased approach identifies a sequence of steps to be completed. In the traditional approach, five developmental components of a project can be distinguished (four steps plus control): initiation, planning and design, execution and construction, monitoring and controlling systems, and completion. Not all projects will have every stage, as projects can be terminated before they reach completion. Some projects do not follow a structured planning and/or monitoring process. And some projects will go through planning and design, execution, and construction multiple times."

"Project Management,"
Wikipedia, accessed January 7, 2013.
http://www.wikipedia.com/projectmanagement.

So project management has as its goal the completion of an improvement project with oversight of the timing to perform the project, the cost of the project, and the quality of the completed project. Cost, time, and quality are the metrics by which we measure the effectiveness of our vendors on one project and collectively with all of their projects.

Not all facilities maintenance projects require full-scale project management. There are projects in which implementation is obvious. These projects don't require planning and design, for the most part. I call these projects call center projects. Examples are when a few lamps are out, the lunch room sheetrock walls need to be painted, the front door handle is broken . . . you get the point. The call comes in from the customer, there is clear understanding as to what the issue is, and no planning or design issues exist. We've experienced many of these issues and know exactly how to address them. For the two companies that I performed facilities management, I would estimate that more than 90 percent of the emergency calls that came in from the customer were call center projects.

Preventative projects, such as servicing HVAC equipment, performing infrared analysis on electrical panels, small sign repairs, etc. are call center-type projects. What these services indicate could lead to project management projects. Predictive projects are nearly all project management-type projects. If your maintenance program has predictive and preventative components, then about 20 percent of all your maintenance projects will involve project management. Some project management projects are very complex and costly. These projects could take months to resolve.

Consider the issue of a sixty-year-old store in downtown Davenport for which we were going to let the lease expire and relocate because the basement took water. If the basement was to be dry, the sump pump had to run continuously. As a result, an elevator and other equipment had deteriorated to the point that they were of no value. The landlord wanted us to solve the basement water entry problem and replace all the deteriorated equipment, which had a price tag of about $200,000. The business unit and the landlord were not budging from their positions.

I hired a local civil engineer to determine the grade of the basement floor; the normal water and flood stage levels of the Mississippi River, which was a half a block away; and what the water levels might have been sixty years ago, considering the development that has taken place since. The engineering report came back and stated that the Mississippi River's normal water level adjacent to this building was a bit higher than the building's basement floor elevation, and the flood stage could get to be six feet above the basement floor. These water levels have risen over the last sixty years due to the amount of development over this time. We issued this report to the landlord and stated that there were existing conditions causing the problem that were beyond our control. Furthermore, the best solution would be to fill in the basement.

A forty-year-old store in California has the electrical service to the building coming from a large retailer's store about 150 feet away. Our electrical panel is about five feet below the main panel in the retailer's store. The mall was doing landscaping repairs, and in the process, a backhoe scraped the galvanized pipe and plastic protective coating off the main electrical feed to our store about twenty feet from our building. No one realized this (supposedly). There was a fire sprinkler line that ruptured underground about fifty feet from the compromised electrical service line. Many gallons of water saturated the ground. Water entered the electrical conduit and poured out onto our store's electrical panel—a very dangerous situation.

It took about a month to ascertain the information I just gave for this issue. We shut the electrical panel off and had to have a generator on site to run the store for that month while many meetings were had with the mall management and the national retailer's management. We finally had all the information to prove who was at fault and responsible for payment. We had to pull out the electrical service cable, reline the inside of the two-inch galvanized pipe, and install a new electrical service cable. The price tag for the improvements and the generator rental was near $50,000. The angst to the store personnel was high. The FMPM who handled this project spent a lot of time almost every day to get this project completed.

Nearly all capital improvement projects are project management in nature—for example, reroofs; parking lot replacements; municipal sewers and water main replacements; structural issues, such as exterior walls, concrete foundations, building supports, and building settlement; HVAC replacements; door replacements; electrical panel replacements; new dumpster or enclosure installation; sign replacements; etc.

Describing those two project management scenarios brought back a sense of the adrenaline that we in facilities maintenance have in dealing with these issues and getting positive resolutions. True excitement is experienced when managing project management projects. When you have a good facilities maintenance team, a good network of national and regional vendors, a handful of good engineers and consultants, and are plugged into all the other areas of expertise needed internally, you feel just about invincible. You don't wish bad or harm to anyone, but you almost feel like saying, "Bring it on!"

Project management projects get the juices flowing. Being able to perform well on these projects separates the good FMPMs from those who want to be. There is a great sense of camaraderie that develops within the facilities maintenance team, because we discuss these projects in our meetings with our vendors and share or whiteboard possible reasons why they occurred and what solutions would work. Facilities maintenance people become fast-twitch people, because there is just so much to do, and we have to keep our A-game on to have the results remain positive consistently. Project management skill sets and competency drive us.

Herding the different types of call center projects will require project management skills. If you do not manage the herd, you could suddenly realize that you are herding cats! Good luck!

Facilities maintenance project managers implement, drive, and oversee the concerns on every project they manage, whether project management issues or call center issues. This position has to have knowledge of the building components—how they are constructed, how they degrade or fail, and how to repair or replace them. They also have to foster relationships with the store managers, district staff, region or zone controllers, and vice presidents; be cognizant of all the management applications stated under the director or manager of facilities maintenance above; be organized to handle many projects at one time with computer data input, filing, follow-ups, and invoicing; attend many meetings; and communicate often with the customers and vendors. Good facilities maintenance project managers are hard to find!

Facilities maintenance project managers are as valuable as any project manager type in a corporate real estate office. The people who realize this most are the ones who do it and those who truly take the time to understand what they do, how they do it, and the results of what they do!

Facilities maintenance project managers *initiate* thousands of projects each year. They will have eighty to 120 active projects at any given time. They initiate national building component capital improvement programs, roofing, parking lots, overhead doors, HVAC, and signs. Upon receiving a request for services from a customer (store manager or district staff), a FMPM will typically initiate the project as follows:

1. Check if store is company-owned or leased.
2. If leased, who is responsible for the building/property maintenance issue?
3. If the landlord is responsible, communicate the building maintenance need with her or him or the property management person, and ask when it will be addressed.
4. If there is a question in the lease as to which party is responsible, then check with the RE legal staff for their review and comment.
5. If the company is responsible, check software data for applicable building component maintenance history, age of building component, store status with operations (any plans to relocate or close the store), any capital expenditures for this building component at this location, and if leased, when the lease expires.

Facilities maintenance project managers have many projects that need to have *plans reviewed* and will interact with architects, engineers, and consultants. They face building foundations issues, exterior wall material failures, issues of drainage (both inside and outside the building), plumbing issues with the municipal sewers (sanitary, storm, and water main), electrical issues with the power supply to the building and within the building, parking lot failures, roofing damage, etc. It is amazing all the different issues that you will face. I can't tell you how many times I've said, "Never seen that before." The large capital projects will have a pre-construction phone conference with the store manager, district assistant manager, contractor representative, contractor project superintendent, and FMPM. They will discuss the nature of the improvement, the project start, where the contractor can place their dumpster, where their workers can park their cars, where the Port-a-Potty will be placed, and any concerns anyone on the call has. Planning and design steps could include the following:

1. Determine if the building problem is known.
   a. Review the construction drawings of the store, and send the applicable sheets to the appropriate vendor or contractor for their review and ability to mark up.
   b. Send appropriate vendor or contractor to the store to inspect the problem and ascertain why the problem exists and what solutions are possible.
   c. Have the vendor or contractor submit a plan or sketch of information determined and photos as needed to best understand the problem that exists.
   d. If needed, have a structural engineering report prepared.
   e. If needed, provide additional engineering information to better understand the site conditions.
2. Determine if we need to repair or replace the building component(s).
   a. If repair is needed, then have a sketch or plan prepared to detail the specifics of the repair.
   b. Determine what materials are allowed to be used.
   c. If replacement is needed, then have a sketch or plan prepared to detail the replacement process and how it will impact the store's operation.

There is a lot of *information that needs to be known* before facilities maintenance project managers can execute the project. The FMPM then has to get three qualified bids either themselves or through the vendor, architect, engineer, or consultant. He or she has to make sure that the awarded contractor performs the improvements at an operating store in a manner that we dictate, not them. Execution and construction steps could include the following:

1. Prepare the bid requests, or provide direction to an approved

building component management company that will prepare the bid requests.

2. Solicit the required bids.
3. Get operation's agreement to proceed.
4. Award the project to the low bidder with a purchase order.
5. Coordinate a pre-construction meeting so that all interested parties are in complete agreement on the scope, timing, and construction procedures.

Facilities maintenance project managers need to be in constant *communication* with the store manager and the vendor that they cut the purchase order with. They will also keep the district staff up to date with many of these projects. They need to make sure that the store is not being negatively impacted by this project. Monitoring and controlling steps could include the following:

1. Get construction progress reports from the contractor.
2. Keep in contact with the store manager and the district staff to make sure there are no disappointments.
3. If anything happens that is different than agreed to in the quote, purchase order, and pre-construction meeting, then a meeting needs to take place to get the reasons why and how the project has been affected.
4. Work with the building component management company or low bidder to keep controls on the project and minimize scope changes.

Completion is the word that a FMPM loves to hear. Completion steps could include the following:

1. Evaluate whether there were any change orders with this project.
2. Make sure the construction site was properly cleaned up.
3. Make sure all construction debris has been properly disposed of.
4. Secure a copy of the sign in/sign out sheet with the store manager's signature signifying that she or he agrees that the project is completed and has no outstanding issues.

5. Enter the completed project information into the facilities maintenance computer system.
6. Approve the invoice, enter information into the computer system, and send for processing.

Facilities maintenance project managers are as capable and valuable as any other project managers in a corporate real estate department. Before we leave the topic of project management, let's look at a typical overview of maintenance project types within a company.

Maintenance Project Types

Operations Department	**Real Estate Department**	
Custodial Maintenance	***Facilities Maintenance***	
Call Center Type	***Call Center Type***	***Project Mgmt Type***
Janitorial	*HVAC minor service*	*HVAC rprs and rplc*
Weekly landscaping	*Door repairs (minor)*	*Door rplc & major rprs*
Security systems	*Exterior sign repairs*	*Sign replacements*
Snow removal		*Elec safety programs,*
		Electrical repairs
		panel replacements,
		and *new installations*
Minor lighting		*New lighting installs*
Minor plumbing		*Major plumbing*
Minor building maint		*Major building maint*
		Roofing rprs & rplc
		Parking lot rprs & rplc
		Structural needs

B. It Takes a Village

Hillary Clinton was right when she said, "It takes a village." Of course, the rest of her statement was, "to raise a child." It does take many other professionals in a corporate office to properly dispatch facilities maintenance services. Let's look at the other professionals that assist the FMPMs to proceed properly with their projects.

Transactions project managers are the leasing experts who have, as their duty, to keep all the stores' leases current and negotiate good lease rates with the landlords in sufficient time (prior to the end of the lease) to enable smooth operation of the stores. On occasion, a lease will be unclear as to who has responsibility for a building component when the FMPM has to address a repair or replacement. The transactions project manager will advise if the company intends to stay at this location, review the lease, and advise who has maintenance responsibility for the building component in question. If the lease is still unclear, they will then take this matter up with a real estate attorney.

The real estate attorneys will review leases and have direct communication with landlord attorneys when the maintenance issues are complex and neither side accepts responsibility. They are also resource experts with plats of surveys, rights of ways, condemnations, lease interpretations, and a host of other issues that arise when maintaining a large portfolio of stores. They are the last line of offense or defense. When the issue is in their hands, they look to us for the business decision direction, but they provide the legal ramifications and offer up their business decision suggestion. The business decision will often be raised up to the vice president of real estate.

Staff members in the design area of real estate have the direction to provide the specifications for new store construction. As such, we look to them to provide us with the specifications for the maintenance services we provide. If our vendors introduce us to an improved product that is cost-effective, we need to provide this information to them for their review and approval. Facilities maintenance will often conclude that a building product is not working as it should and make recommendations for a new product to take its place. We certainly want to be in conformance with the design areas specifications so that, to the best of our ability, there is uniformity between the new stores and existing stores.

Facilities maintenance will many times work in concert with the refresh, reimage, or remodel program that is coordinated by the construction area of real estate. We will schedule the reroof projects, parking lot improvements, and overhead door replacements to be performed before the refresh, reimage, or remodel projects take place. We will collaborate with them on vendors, contractors, building component products, and contract terms.

We have a large budget. We perform many projects. We spend a lot of the company's money. We have many invoices. All financial issues are coordinated with and in conformance with the accounting area of real estate. They are the capital or expense referees. They assist with the monthly reporting of spending and YE spending estimates with management.

FMPMs need to know which projects the environmental experts of the real estate department will coordinate. These projects will include soil contamination, mold, animal infestation, oil spill issues, and hazardous material disposal, including disposal of fluorescent lamps. On occasion, other issues occur at the same time, and we need to coordinate our efforts with them.

FMPMs will work with loss prevention project managers when health or safety issues exist. Many times these occasions occur during emergency events, such as hurricanes, tornados, flooding, and the like. They will help frame the scope of services needed and provide the direction to proceed. They will contact us with any other maintenance issue that could cause harm—a roof leak causing a trip and fall potential, a pothole in the parking lot that could cause a trip and fall, an eye wash station in the car shop area that is not working properly, doors that are not working properly and cannot properly lock, etc.

FMPMs will also have interactions on occasion with purchasing, IT, human resources, and marketing. You can understand why it is appropriate to say that in order to have a facilities maintenance area functioning properly, "It takes a village."

C. Customer Service

This is where it all starts. Our customers are the store managers, district staff, the controllers, and region or zone VPs. This group of people makes up the operations department. Their charge is to sell our company's products and services to the paying customer—the boss. We need to provide our services to them, thereby helping them be successful; foster positive in-store morale for our teammates; and help the boss to have a positive experience and return to our store.

I searched for the term *customer service* and was sent to Wikipedia. I received three pages of information. The following are portions of this response:

[8]"Customer service is an organization's ability to supply its customers' wants and needs. If we're going to consistently exceed customers' expectations, we have to recognize that every aspect of our business has an impact on customer service. Improving customer service involves making a commitment to learning what our customers' needs and wants are and developing action plans that implement customer-friendly processes.

Eight Rules for Good Customer Service

1. Answer your phone. Answer the customer's call or e-mail as soon as possible. Don't be in the habit of putting your phone off the hook because you are too busy!
2. Don't make promises unless you will keep them—not *plan* to keep them but *will* keep them. Reliability is one of the keys to any good relationship, and good customer service is no exception. Think before you give any promise, because nothing annoys customers more than a broken one.
3. Listen to your customers. Is there anything more exasperating than telling someone what you want or what your problem is and then discovering that that person hasn't been paying attention and needs to have it explained again? Let your customer talk, and show him or her that you are listening by making the appropriate responses, such as suggesting how to solve the problem.
4. Deal with complaints. No one likes hearing complaints, and many of us have developed a reflex shrug, saying, "You can't please all the people all the time." Maybe not, but if you give the complaint your attention, you may be able to please this

one person this one time and position your relationship to reap the benefits of good customer service.

5. Be helpful, even if there's no immediate profit in it. Do a good deed, and the customer will spread the word of what you have done for her or him.

6. Train your staff to always be helpful, courteous. and knowledgeable. Talk with them about good customer service regularly.

7. Take the extra step. Whatever the extra step may be, if you want to provide good customer service, take it. They may not say so to you, but people notice when you make an extra effort and will tell other people.

8. Throw in something extra. Don't think that an act or statement has to be large to be effective."

"Customer Service,"
Wikipedia, accessed January 7, 2013.
http://www.wikipedia.com/customerservice

You can't cut corners on customer service. Check out people who provide customer service. See what they are doing, and go to school—learn it, and then do it. Observe a good waitress or waiter at a restaurant or a good salesperson at a store. You know when you experience good customer service; you feel that the person took his or her time with you and cared about you, and it felt good!

If you provide good customer service, it will pay dividends in your position as a facilities maintenance project manager. It actually makes the job more fun, because now the job is not just about building components, but also about people!

D. Communication

Communication is a key component of the quality of a project. There are many people to communicate with—store managers, district staff, region or zone controllers, vendors and contractors, landlords, all the internal areas listed above, and the director or manager of facilities maintenance. The different forms of communication are e-mail, phone, meetings, conference calls, reports, and face-to-face. Don't forget to use your phone. There is a place for a direct conversation.

Don't assume anything in this position. It is best to discuss an issue and get clear understanding. Disappointment, anger, meetings you don't want to be in—noise—can all be avoided in most cases with the proper communication. This is a key component to customer service. It is better to overdo it than to sell it short.

Always be accessible for phone calls and/or meetings with the customer. It will pay dividends now and in the future.

E. Organization

In the wake of all the projects a FMPM completes is paperwork. Organize it! Make sure the project files are complete with all the necessary documents so that anyone going to the files to see what took place on the project has clear information of what transpired. Data that has to be entered into the project tracking system or databases has to be accurate and entered during the project and especially at the completion of the project. This data will be the history that enables us to make better decisions in the future. Your desk will certainly be a mess on occasion when things are overwhelming. I've been there and done that many times! However, the overarching goal has to be to have an organized desk area. Have a place for everything, and know where everything is. This position is so fast-paced that you can't lose time looking for something. Look at your desk area as a picture of how people see your ability to think through an issue.

Keep up with your project follow-ups! This is the main management tool that drives a project to completion. Don't be sloppy with this detail. Use it, and be successful. Don't use it, and you will need more excuses than you can imagine for why you didn't get that project completed. All someone has to do is to check on your follow-ups, and if they are nonexistent, you lose credibility.

Attend all meetings, and be prepared to discuss your projects. Be a team player, and be an active participant in this process. People want to hear what issues you have and how you addressed them, because after all, we can all learn from each other. Don't be a lone ranger!

Be positive; don't be a whiner. There are times to have a one-on-one conversation with the director or manager of facilities maintenance to let her or him know your concerns, but it is never good to complain to the group on a consistent basis. When one member of a facilities maintenance staff is not pulling his or her weight, he or she makes it a drag for the rest of the team. My suggestion is that if a task is too darn hard, then leave the area or company. If this situation persists, it is just a matter of time before you will be fired.

It has been my experience that if a person is well-organized and performs all his or her functions well, there will not be an employee issue. Consequently, when the FMPM is not organized and does not perform all her or his functions well, there will be an employee issue. It's pretty transparent.

The moral of the story is to be organized. Listen to management as to what is expected, and meet those expectations. What's really noticed is if you better those expectations. If management sees an employee performing with no perceived guard rails that define his or her position and continually exceeds expectations, it doesn't take long before he or she is rewarded.

F. Inspection of Properties and Projects

After we developed the predictive and preventative maintenance program at Company B, the three of us in the facilities maintenance area took two branch inspection trips a month. These trips were usually three to four days in length. We would take about four hours to inspect a branch. This inspection would be a thorough walk-through of the property and building. We would interview the store manager to determine what concerns she or he had about the maintenance and operation of the branch.

We would have one of our area contractors accompany us on many of these trips. They were a great resource to answer questions and get information on building conditions. We also would set up seminars for us to attend to get education we needed to better understand the building conditions we would find. For example, one such seminar was a trip to a local block manufacturer. This seminar taught us that there are three types of concrete masonry units (blocks)—light weight, middle weight, and heavy weight. They showed us samples of each and ran water through each. It was extremely educational. We also discussed the weatherproofing aspects of each block and what paints or stains are used to provide waterproofing. Knowing what you are looking at when you inspect building components is extremely beneficial!

These inspections were one of the highlights of the position. You would walk the building, see the problems, and get very good at knowing the cause of the problems. On occasions, I would have a middle-level management person accompany me on an inspection trip. One time, the information systems vice president joined me. While we were inspecting a roof, I said to the roofing system, "Uncle Al is here; show me where you are hurting."

This VP, who was a lot of fun to have on the trip, said, "You are weird." I got to the point where I couldn't help myself; wherever I go, I always look at building components, notice maintenance needs, and surmise what improvements are needed.

That was a disappointment, of sorts, when I came to Company A; there wasn't a facilities maintenance inspection program. Due to the large number of stores and the limited staff, we were unable to institute one. We had to rely on the vendors to supply pictures and plans of what they saw. I believe that a facilities maintenance person should have the opportunity to inspect the buildings that she or he responsible to maintain. The added advantage is that you get to meet the customer and hear firsthand what his or her issues are. In a situation where you can't inspect stores, you better have very good vendors and contractors. And we did! They still do!

VII

VENDORS

Approximately three people in top management, six people in middle management, and five people in the facilities maintenance area have fulfilled the management direction and application for the company's facilities maintenance program. Management of performance is next to be fulfilled. This aspect of management will require thousands of people. This army of technicians and contractors will be supervised by our national and regional top eleven vendors. Their performance will be anxiously watched and commented on by hundreds or thousands of people—our store managers and their teammates.

Picture going to a home game of your city's NFL team, but instead of seeing your favorite professional football team, you will see your company's facility maintenance program at play. Top-level management is the owner of the facilities maintenance program. They are present in the owner suites, way above the elevation of the football field. Middle-level management is in nearby suites. The head coach of your facilities maintenance network of vendors is the director of facilities maintenance. The assistant coaches are the FMPMs. Together, they manage the activity of the network of vendors. Our team on the field is the network of vendors that we have selected to perform our facilities maintenance program. The opposing team on the field is the maintenance needs of your stores—deferred, emergency, and life cycle maintenance. The home fans are the store managers and district managers. The opposing fans are our competitors, who don't want to see our stores maintained.

Do you see the importance of the performance? Our national and regional vendors are on the field of play. They face a tough opponent. There is a packed stadium of highly interested spectators—the store managers, district managers, controllers, region or zone VPs, real estate VP, COO, CFO, and president.

The coaching staff is under great pressure to win. We have to have qualified vendors who know our aspects of management and perform within our company's management direction and application. They have to manage their approved technicians and subcontractors to perform as they direct, with cost efficiency, timing conformance, and quality of workmanship.

Finally, we all have to hear the cheers of the crowd, which is full of people who are satisfied with the performance of their facilities maintenance program. If we push back the deferred maintenance, address the emergency projects, and implement life cycle building component replacements as desired by our fans, we will hear their cheers. Otherwise, we will hear *boos*.

Just as your local NFL team has to make changes when the fans continually *boo* its performance, changes will be made to get the right vendors, and if need be, the right coaches if the maintenance program does not satisfy our customers.

A. Sense of Duty

A vendor or contractor is selected to perform a company's building component facilities maintenance improvements after winning a very competitive bidding process. The selected party needs to be very cognizant that there are many other companies that want to be in its position. It behooves this party to know that it is part of the facilities maintenance team, and as such, the people need to know exactly what is expected of them in order to meet or exceed expectations. As shown in the analogy above, we operate in a fish bowl. Our results are highly visible and quickly disseminated. We need to consistently win the management of performance.

The facilities maintenance staff has entrusted your company with getting positive results. Positive results ensure that the work was performed in accordance with the plans, specs, quote, and/or purchase order; the cost of the project was competitive with the right scope of work; the timing of the project was proper and considerate of the store personnel; and the quality of the work performed including excellent communication with the store and real estate personnel. In addition, good workmanship that left the work area clean and all refuse properly disposed of is a must. This type of service needs to be performed for every project over and over again.

The vendor or contractor has to provide ongoing reporting of his or her activity and present updated reports at our monthly meetings. All of the vendor's or contractor's employees who are active with our projects need to be present at our monthly conference calls to discuss any projects that are having difficulty or noise issues. Also, those vendors or contractors that are required to maintain a database of their completed repairs and replacements of the building component they manage have to keep the information current. A lot is required of an approved vendor or contractor.

If the vendor or contractor is not willing to provide these services or keep up with them, then we will interview other companies to find a replacement. The facilities maintenance staff is under pressure to perform and meet the needs of the customer each and every time she or he calls. We can't be joined to vendors or contractors that don't conform to our application management.

We receive direction management from top—and middle-level management. As a result, we develop the application management that will be utilized to carry out the facilities maintenance program. The approved vendors and contractors have to receive and understand the application management and then provide this direction to their approved technicians and subcontractors. We don't allow the work to be passed on to a third party. The reason for this is twofold; first, the translation of what's required gets diluted, and second, we don't want to pay three markups for one project. In this way, we better guarantee proper communication with and conformance to the application management and are more cost-efficient for the work performed.

The vendors and contractors then have to monitor the work being performed. They need to be aware of the work their companies provide to our customers. If the work is a call center-type project, it will take less involvement then a project management-type project. Regardless, they need to be the managers of the project and the results and not let a technician or subcontractor have this role. The technicians performing the work don't interact directly with us, our vendor's company's' coordinator or project manager do. Oversight is extremely important, regardless of what type of project it is.

Know that you are on the field of performance and that everyone is watching. It is best to know what is expected of you and be willing and able to perform in this environment and win. The facilities maintenance staff is a partner with you and wants you to succeed. Enter the competition to be competitive in all aspects of your performance. Enjoy the victories. This job can be rewarding if you are competent, trustworthy, a good teammate, and ready to perform at a high level.

B. Our _____ Building Component Management Company

There is a great team of vendors and contractors at the Company A. I will share how they operate so that you better understand the term *management company*. We had a minimum of three-year contracts with all of these vendors or contractors.

Roofing Vendor

The roofing vendor is a roofing manufacturer company. It has a building owner services area. This area provides emergency leak response services. I stated above the unit code/unit cost management principal that allows us to proceed quickly to address our customers' needs. The average leak call cost is approximately $1,100; therefore, we didn't need bids. The customer could select a local roofing contractor to go and address this leak.

Emergency projects had a four-hour response time. Non-emergencies had a twenty-four—to forty-eight-hour response time. When the company went to inspect one of our roofs for leaks, we wanted its employees to inspect the entire roof and advise us if there were other roof repairs needed, thereby allowing us to save repair costs later and better assure that we would get the life cycle of the roofing system. In this way, we wanted the company to be our roofing component management company. Their employees were not just contractors. They were our partners in addressing the needs of our roofs with proper oversight and in a cost-effective manner.

Sometimes these emergency leak calls would lead to more expensive roof repairs. The quoted repairs would require individual line items listing all the specific repairs required with the unit listed and a price provided. If all these costs were over $10,000, we had to get two bids. The average area of our stores was approximately eight thousand square feet. Because the roof area was not that large, we rarely exceeded the $10,000 threshold.

At other times, these emergency leak calls would lead to the recommendation for a reroof. We also had a life cycle reroofing program. For both reroofing project types, we would request a roof condition analysis. This report would have a sketch of the roof, showing the pitch of the roof, the drains, all units on the roof, and the dimensions of the roof areas. There would be pictures and recommendations for improvements with the estimated cost. We also had cores taken, when applicable, to determine if there was asbestos present. Our roofing building component management company would prepare the project specifications and send the project out to three qualified roofing contractors within close proximity of our store.

The FMPM would review the submitted three-bid analysis report. She or he would evaluate the scope of the project and associated costs to determine if they were in line with our spending trends for these projects. The FMPM would then submit this project information to the director of facilities maintenance for his review and approval. After his review and approval, he would then submit the project paperwork to management for its review and approval.

Once all the approvals were received, the FMPM would then issue a purchase order to our roofing building component management company. The company would then issue a contract to the low bidder. At this point, our roofing component management company would set up a pre-construction meeting phone conference with the store manager, the assistant district manager, the roof contractor spokesman, the roof contractor superintendent, the company itself, and the appropriate FMPM. The objective of this meeting was to ensure that all the project information was understood by all interested parties. The finished roofing project was then inspected by the roofing vendor's technician to make sure that it was properly installed and in conformance with the project specifications.

When our roofing vendor project managers were satisfied that the project was properly completed and they had all the needed paperwork from the roofing contractor, they submitted the invoice for the project to the FMPM.

This vendor was responsible to maintain a database of reroof projects and be able to forecast what roofs were recommended to be reroofed within the next five-year period. The vendor also had to maintain a project tracking report of all its activity during a current year. Finally, the vendor attended a bimonthly red meeting so our teams could go over the activity.

As I stated above, we would go to our vendors and contractors for a three-day seminar. During this time, our _____ building component management company would download its knowledge to our facilities maintenance team. In this way, our team became educated about that building component. These were also great team-building events.

This company had access to over two thousand roofing contractors and probably used over two hundred companies each year to service our roofing needs.

Parking Lots Vendor

The parking lot vendor is a paving contractor. This paving contractor has a working relationship with quarries and material supply yards around the country. We had a number of different resources for this work, but this particular company kept performing well and wanted to handle additional areas of the country. Over the course of a number of years, the company eventually became our main resource for this work across the country. It had a team of people who manage parking lot projects for corporations. These projects could be anywhere in the United States.

The average cost of a minor parking lot improvement—striping, pothole repair, handicap signage, etc.—would be $1,500 or less. The average cost of a substantial patching project would be $5,000-8,000. As such, if we had detailed line items for all the work required and the unit costs were in line, we didn't need to get bids.

If an FMPM had a call from a store manager requesting parking lot improvements, he or she would get the best understanding of their issue over the phone. The FMPM would then determine all the information that we have on this parking lot and provide all of this information to our parking lots building component management company for its review and handling. If repairs were needed, the company would submit the proper project paperwork for our review and approval. The response times for parking lot surveys were two days for emergencies and five days for non-emergencies.

If this survey resulted in a parking lot mill and pave or replacement, then there would be a detailed process put in place to assure the right improvement is made in the quickest time period. See a copy of Parking Lot > $25,000 Project Process in Appendix C. This capital improvement project would also have a pre-construction meeting phone conference. This meeting would be absolutely necessary to insure that all interested parties knew what the scope of the project was, the timing of the start date and the anticipated completion date for the project, what communications were necessary with the store manager, who the contractor's superintendent was, how the project was phased, where they could park, where the Port-a-Potty would be placed, and that no asphalt contractor was allowed to walk into the store.

This vendor was nearing completion of a database of all the parking lot improvements it had coordinated for us. The vendor would soon have to also provide a five-year projection of recommended parking lot replacement projects. The vendor submitted reporting of all its activity for use and was responsible to attend a monthly red meeting to go over its projects.

This company had access to over one thousand parking lot contractors and probably used over two hundred companies each year to service our parking lot needs.

HVAC Equipment Vendor

This building component was the first national building component program I developed for Company A. The year 2012 was the ninth year of its relationship with Company A. This vendor was primarily involved with HVAC units, heaters, and exhaust fans. It had a call center program with the stores; the stores could contact the vendor directly for service. If this service was below a NTE, they could deliver the needed service immediately. If over the NTE amount, the HVAC vendor's project managers needed to submit a proposal for the repairs. The appropriate FMPM will then review the proposal and submit a purchase order. The service work that is below the NTE is invoiced on a bulk purchase order to the director of facilities maintenance. This work is done fast and paid fast.

This vendor was required to have a database of all the HVAC equipment and supply a five-year projection for replacements based on the life cycle and condition of the equipment. A life cycle program is in place for the replacement of HVAC units. The vendor also has project tracking reporting of all its service calls. It has spending reports that keep a tally of where we are at with capital and expense spending. Because this building component has the propensity to have the most noise, we agreed to meet weekly to go over the complex projects. The vendor has nine people regularly on these calls. Things go so well with this building component that these calls are usually fifteen minutes long.

We also have a program to address the problematic heaters. By having these life cycle programs and the store direct call center for service calls, there are not a lot of calls from the stores for repairs to the FMPMs.

If a replacement project is complex, then a pre-construction phone conference is held, similar to those held for roofs and parking lots. Because the usual HVAC units are either five-ton or 7.5-ton units and the unit cost is generally under $10,000, bids are not required. The costs from this vendor have to be in conformance with the contract. The paperwork flow is similar to that for roofs.

This vendor stepped up its service to us when it dedicated three project managers to address the difficult projects. These three individuals—one each in Newark, Atlanta, and Dallas—are seasoned HVAC experts. They are the heavy hitters who fly anywhere in their region to address issues that get stagnated due to complexity. They really address the concept that they are our HVAC building component project management company. The response times for HVAC service were four hours for emergencies and twenty-four to forty-eight hours for non-emergencies.

This company self-performed with its own technicians for about 25 percent of the country and utilized about two hundred companies to address our needs in the rest of the country.

Passage Doors and Windows and Repair Garage Doors

There are many passage doors, windows, and garage doors at Company A's stores. A good building component project management company for these services is a must. There are hundreds of direct phone calls from the store managers to this company to service these building components for Company A; 95 percent of these work requests are call center type. These repairs or part replacements happen in a hurry. The direct phone calls from customer to service provider save time. The bulk invoice process speeds up payment for these services. We demanded a lot from our vendors to perform at their peak potential; therefore, we should do nothing less to get them payment for services well rendered.

When a vendor primarily operates in a call center-type project mode, it is very important that its people recognize immediately when they have ventured into a project management-type project mode. In these cases, it is not just a matter of finding the right technician or subcontractor to do the needed work and manage their performance. Now they need to put on their thinking caps and view the project from all angles. Information needs to be gathered, reasons for the building component failure need to be determined, and options for improvements need to be formulated. This is a great service to a corporate real estate department when a vendor can perform well in both the call center-type mode and the project management-type mode.

This vendor embraced the building component management company with suggestions for parts improvements that not only functioned better but were also less costly than the specified parts. The vendor's aggressiveness to continually improve our specifications was a clear indication that it valued being a partner with us to provide high-quality facilities maintenance to our customers.

This vendor stepped up its service capability by improving its reporting of its activities both for the facilities maintenance projects and for the custodial maintenance projects that it performed for the operations department. The vendor also had just put forth an improved project tracking software that would allow our FMPMs to go to its website to view live data on the status of a project. The vendor's employees were active in attending our monthly red meetings and would occasionally fly out to our office to attend these meetings in person. The response time for their emergency projects was four hours and for non-emergency projects was next-day.

This company had access to over two thousand door and window contractors and probably used over 250 companies each year to service our door and window needs.

Garage Doors

I bid this program out to three national overhead door companies. We had a great relationship with the company that won this bidding process. We replaced hundreds of overhead doors per year. We did this with lightning speed due to the unit code/unit cost management process. The specs, operations, and appearances were uniform for these doors. The new store specs were revised to have this company also provide the doors for the new stores. We liked to have three-inch channels installed when we could to provide a sturdier functioning for the doors. Fifty thousand cycle springs were specified for the same reason. The astragal was also improved for durability.

The company we used also provided a great service to address any problems that arose. They didn't happen often, but when they did, we had them analyzed and fixed. These doors are crucial to the operation of the bays.

Our facilities maintenance team also visited the vendor's plant and saw the manufacturing process. It was very impressive. This company had great reporting to track the progress of the projects, the list of completed projects, and spending YTD. The employees had an Excel spreadsheet of all the doors they installed for us. They provided a turnkey installation process for us. In this way, qualified garage door installers put these doors into operation. This type of service greatly reduced the noise issues we had with these installations. They were diligent to attend our red meetings on a monthly basis and were prepared with the up-to-date reports of their activity.

This company had access to over two thousand garage door installers and probably used over 100 companies each year to service our garage door needs.

Electrical Safety Programs and Service

We had two electrical safety programs; one was called electrical panels, and the other was called electrical branch. The electrical panels program included the following services: the infrared analysis of the electrical panels at a store once every five years, check the building ground, and perform a breaker test. The infrared report would show heat spots that indicated that improvements were needed: tighten loose wire connections, replace defective breakers, replace defective buss bars, replace defective panels, etc. The breaker test would indicate if the breaker was actually defective, allowing all current to pass through it. These breakers would be replaced. This program was put in place to be reoccurring forever.

The electrical branch program included the following services: make sure all outlets were properly grounded, make sure all outlets were three-hole pronged, and hardwire any improper extension cord use. This was a one-time five-year program that would end after performing this improvement to every store.

I bid this program out to two companies. Both companies performed the service well, and their costs were both very competitive. The only difference was that one company had a very good website that would track the data of all these inspections. This company has the best website for tracking their services of any of the vendors I used. Every breaker within every panel was labeled during this work, and this information was loaded into the computer database. The database also shows what types of panels are present.

This company also addresses all the electrical service calls. It is a great resource to our customers to respond quickly with accurate data in-hand before the technician even arrives at the store. Safety is maximized with these types of electrical programs and service in place.

This company administers the electrical programs and is up to date with information at the monthly red meetings. Its emergency service time is two hours, and its non-emergency time is five days.

This company had access to over two thousand electrical contractors and probably used over two hundred companies each year to service our electrical needs.

Lighting

We bid out the lighting program to three companies in late 2003. This is when we began to remove the T-12 lamps and magnetic ballasts from the stores. We completed the lighting program improvements to every store in 2010. Now all the stores have T-8 lamps with electronic ballasts. It was great to remove all the magnetic PCB's ballasts. The lighting is much better, and the energy savings are great. We are now in a caretaking process with these new lamps and ballasts.

The company that performed these improvements had all the improvements entered into a database. This database lists every room in each store and shows the type and number of each fixture, the type and number of each ballast, and the type and number of each lamp.

The company that provides the caretaking process for these lighting systems has access to over 1,500 lighting contractors and will use about three hundred companies each year to service our lighting needs.

General Contractors

We had two national and regional general contractors under contract. There were also a number of regional and area contractors approved to be used for our maintenance work. These more local contractors did not have multi-year contracts. Therefore, a purchase order was needed for every project they performed.

We utilized general contractors when the building component didn't have enough activity to warrant a vendor to just address that one issue. The type of building components that were mostly handled by general contractors were exterior walls; interior improvements to floors, walls, and ceilings, plumbing improvements; construction of storage areas or dumpsters; installing fencing; metal roofing repairs; and structural improvements.

Utilizing the unit code/unit cost management tool allowed us to proceed quickly to address the customer's needs. But when the project cost was over $10,000, we had to get three bids. Having a bullpen of approved general contractors to bid our projects allowed us to operate with an understanding of approved specifications, history of what we did at other locations, and uniform pricing. These factors assisted us in being highly successful with the cost, timing, and quality of these completed projects.

The two contracted general contractors had great reporting of their activity and brought qualified and energetic personnel into the positions of managing their work with us. These two companies would address emergency issues within two to four hours and non-emergency issues within twenty-four to forty-eight hours.

Each of these companies has access to more than two thousand contractors and used more than three hundred companies each year to service our general contracting needs.

Exterior Signage

The construction area of real estate had the responsibility to contract for this service. The reason for this is because those in construction oversaw the activity of the new store's construction signage and the rebranding signage program. Due to this activity, they wanted three sign companies to serve the country. The maintenance area could have done well with just two companies, but we aligned the servicing of our signage maintenance needs with the alignment of these three sign companies regionally as determined by the construction company.

All three of these companies truly cared for the sign maintenance they provided. They provided weekly update reports of their activity and attended monthly red meetings to discuss difficult projects and how their sign maintenance program was progressing.

Each of these three companies has access to more than 1,500 sign installation contractors and used more than two hundred companies each year to service our sign needs.

With the four FMPMs and I who made up the corporate facilities maintenance team and the above referenced national and regional vendors and contractors, I had no problem walking onto the field of facilities maintenance play each and every day. We collectively addressed thousands of projects a year. We managed thousands of call center-type projects and experienced a wide variety of project management-type projects.

I never felt we were in over our heads. If we needed other expertise to provide direction, we had that also. There was a great team of professionals internally at our disposal. Like I stated above, I thought, *Bring it on!*

That's why we could enter the field of play knowing that we would push back our opponents: deferred maintenance, emergency projects, and life cycle replacements. Some days, I felt roughed up, but I never felt defeated. Eventually, the project would be completed to everyone's satisfaction. If a customer ever complained about a finished project, we would circle the wagons, and the vendor would have to inspect the finished work, find out what did not get done correctly, and make the correction.

This type of maintenance program maximized the following:

- relationships with the national/regional vendors
- databasing completed work
- proper tracking of all projects
- communication between the customer, vendor, and appropriate FMPM
- respect between all participants
- making the right repair or replacement decision

- ability to stay within the overall facilities maintenance budget
- detailed monthly reporting of the projects and dollars to upper management
- keeping track of the spending with the real estate accounting area
- putting the needs of the customer above everything else
- working hard and enjoying the accomplishments of each individual and the group
- appreciating the hard work and efficiency of our vendors and contractors

C. Handling the Two Project Types

There are two types of projects that vendors and contractors will handle for their corporate customers—call center-type projects and project management-type projects. A more direct discussion of these two project types and how they should be handled needs to be had.

Call Center-Type Projects

Call center-type projects are customer requests that require little to no fact-finding or analysis of the problem or putting forth options for improvements. Typically, the repair or replacement decision is obvious. It is a simple decision and requires only one phone call to a technician. The typical cost for these projects will range from $300-800. The vendor or contractor coordinator contacts his or her technician or the selected subcontractor to go to the store to address the issue and make the immediate repair or replacement. Some of these projects are replacing burned-out lamps, fixing restroom fixtures, plumbing pipe flow repairs, door repairs, minor HVAC repairs, or minor general contracting services (painting, floor repairs, ceiling repairs).

If you are reading this book and have gotten this far, you are well aware of these type of projects. I always wanted to work directly with the vendor or contractor who handled the building component in need so that if he or she did not self-perform, the project only got subbed out one time. The vendor would contact a subcontractor to provide the service for this maintenance issue. This contacted subcontractor was not allowed to then contact another company to do the work for it.

If the project was handed off to a third party, then our company paid three mark-ups. This wasn't necessary. Misunderstandings and mistakes are minimized if the vendor or contractor's coordinator doesn't just contact the subcontractor and pass this project to her or him but rather remains engaged as the lead person on the project. This also allows the contractor to see how the issue was handled, what communications were had with the store manager, if the right materials were used, and whether the finished project is acceptable with the store manager.

It is tempting for these coordinators to simply pass this project off to the subcontractor and let him or her handle it as he or she sees fit. After all, is this person not the competent, trained professional who can do this work and thereby doesn't need to be told what to do? However, the subcontractors do need to be told how they will act, what materials they will use, and that they won't be paid unless the store manager is satisfied with the completed work. Yes, the subcontractor has the talent to use the wrench, so to speak—that's why she or he was contacted—but this person needs to know the direction and application aspects of management. That's what you, the vendor or contractor coordinator, should be well versed in. Keep control of these projects, and don't be intimidated by prima donna technicians or contractors who don't want to be guided by you.

Project Management-Type Projects

Let me state the obvious: these are not call center-type projects. Don't treat them as such. There was a detailed discussion of project management for the FMPMs. There were five developmental components that were listed and explained. Let's have this discussion for vendors and contractors.

Initiation If you are a valued partner with the corporate real estate facilities maintenance team, you will receive the baton of performance for many projects. You should initiate the project management-type project as follows:

1. Get a download of information about this store's building component(s) issues from the FMPM.
2. Get clear direction from the FMPM as to what he or she perceives the issue(s) to be and how he or she wants you to proceed.
3. Direct your in-house technician or contractor or a selected subcontractor to go to the store and do a thorough inspection of the problem(s).
4. Interview the store manager and other teammates who can give information on the problem: when it started, how it affects the business of the store, what might have caused it.
5. Develop a clear understanding of the problem(s), get them in writing, and provide corresponding photos of these areas.
6. Develop a clear understanding of what caused the problem(s), get them in writing, and provide corresponding photos of these areas.

Planning and Design
1. Review the construction plans that the FMPM provided.
2. Recommend engineering evaluation if needed.
3. Develop the plans or sketch necessary to clearly define what improvements are proposed.
4. If practical, provide alternate improvement approaches.
5. Provide a detailed item list of improvements needed with descriptions, units of improvements, and unit costs and a subtotal cost for that line item's improvement.
6. Provide total of the cost of all the line item subtotals.
7. Clearly define the materials to be used.
8. Issue your proposal for the improvements to the FMPM.

Execution and Construction If you are awarded with the purchase order to proceed with the work, then proceed as follows:

1. Assign who will perform these improvements—your in-house techs or contractors or a subcontracting company.
2. Regardless of who will perform these improvements, provide them the application processes in place by the real estate

department and impress upon them that they will be followed.

3. Provide them the plans and specifications for the project, and go over it with them.
4. If a pre-construction phone conference will be held for this project, demand that they be present.
5. Make it clear to them that they answer to you, and they will correct anything found not acceptable by you, the store manager, or the FMPM.
6. Make sure they proceed as stated in the approved plans and specifications and that the correct materials are used.
7. Provide construction oversight as needed.

Monitoring and Controlling Systems Make sure that you are satisfied that the project is progressing properly.

1. Keep the store manager updated on the progress of the project, and ask if there are any problems with the project.
2. Keep the FMPM updated on the project status and whether there are any issues with the store manager.
3. Advise the FMPM if the project is not being performed as planned and if anyone gets hurt on the project.
4. Keep the status reports up-to-date on all active projects.
5. Make sure that the construction area is being properly cleaned up at the end of each day.
6. Make sure that the construction refuse is being properly stored and removed from the store.
7. Address concerns immediately with the FMPM, not at the end of the project.

Completion
1. Make sure that all the work has been completed in accordance with the purchase order.
2. Make sure that the construction site has been cleaned up and is acceptable with the store manager.

3. Make sure that all construction debris has been properly cleaned up.
4. Make sure that the sign in/sign out sheet has been properly reviewed and signed by the store manager.
5. Communicate all of these developments with the FMPM.
6. Enter the completed project information into your company's reports and database (if applicable).
7. Submit the invoice with the following:
   a. Copy of the purchase order
   b. Progress and completion photos
   c. Copy of the completed sign in/sign out sheet
   d. Copy of all applicable warranties
   e. Any change order forms
   f. Any germane communication during this project

Project management projects are complex and involve all the activity listed above. There is a great difference between these types of projects and call center-type projects. Know when a project needs project management oversight, and perform it with the detail demanded.

D. Project Tracking, Reporting, Database Entries, and Meetings

If you can't follow through with this detail, communication, and interaction with the real estate facilities maintenance team, then all your good construction work will not save the relationship. You have to be able to complete the package—be a full-service vendor or contractor. These things are needed by the facilities maintenance team to keep us in the know and help us to better manage what you are doing for us. You can't manage what you can't see.

Ongoing project tracking allows us to see what is transpiring on a project at any point in time. The updated reports allow us to see all of your activity for us at any point during the year. This information is critical during our monthly or more frequent meetings. If a database is in affect that allows us to better determine the life cycle replacement projects for each year, then keeping this information up-to-date is also critical. We all have to be detailed to win the corporate maintenance game. The other vendors do it; you don't want to be the weak link. The relationship will be strained this way. This job can be enjoyable and successes celebrated if we are all on the same page. Remember, the customer is right. Give the customer what he or she wants. The facilities maintenance customer needs this detail.

VIII

OPERATIONS DEPARTMENT

A. Needs

Being a qualified director or manager of facilities maintenance, you know what the ultimate needs are for the maintenance of the company's properties and stores. The direction of what facilities maintenance program is approved and funded comes from top- and middle-level management. The director or manager of facilities maintenance will be knowledgeable of the difference between the ultimate needs and those that are funded. One thing the director or manager of facilities maintenance should do is to provide statistical information to top- and middle-level management of the additional facilities maintenance needs and determine if there are additional funds available to address some of these unmet needs. One thing the director or manager of facilities maintenance must do is put together the application processes and direction to maximize the facilities maintenance that can be performed with the budget provided.

Now we are ready to acknowledge and receive the facilities maintenance needs. Many of the needs will be understood from building component databases and the resultant life cycle reports that dictate the locations for recommended replacements. If there are no databases, then they will be developed on an ongoing basis with the completed replacement projects. Over time, the needed databases will be developed. Other day-to-day needs will be received from our customers—the store managers and district staff. These needs are, in most cases, emergencies.

The facilities maintenance team now has all the needs receptacles activated. Its members have developed the application processes. The selection of the team of vendors and contractors needed to meet the facilities maintenance needs is an extremely important task, because this group of companies will be joined with the facilities maintenance team to meet the customer's needs.

Now the facilities maintenance team is open for business to provide the service needed to meet our customers' requested and perceived facilities maintenance needs. We will meet these needs as far as the budget will allow. When we receive the calls for service, we respond, as we want to provide the customers a professional response. We show them respect all through the process and provide quality vendors and contractors to perform the work required.

B. Results

Store managers and their teammates, district staff, controllers, and region or zone operations VPs make up the group of people within the company that sell the service and/or products that are the core business of the company. It is that portion of the company that generates incoming cash. These people are all about results. When I got to work in the morning, I was greeted by a flat screen with the company's sales results by zone from the previous day.

The competition between zones and districts and stores is incredible. Maintenance expenditures detract from the bottom-line profit figure. This book's main attempt was to prove the value of maintenance expenditures and how they are not direct losses but actually support the marketing and operations of the stores.

Our customers are very knowledgeable about costs, spending, and profits. They are results-oriented. We need to value their input and feedback on all we do. Their questions are:

1. Are the facilities maintenance costs competitive?
2. Are the vendors and contractors competent?
3. Is the work that was done in conformance with the approved purchase order?

4. Shouldn't the work area be cleaned better than it was?
5. Was the construction debris allowed to be thrown in the store's dumpster?
6. Was the project done properly?

We need to ask them questions as well:

1. Was the work performed done well?
2. Do you have any concerns with the completed project?
3. Was the vendor or contractor professional throughout the project?
4. Did the vendor or contractor communicate with you throughout the project?
5. Was there anything that could have been done better?

All of this input and feedback is critical to a successful facilities maintenance program. The operations department will provide feedback on the facilities maintenance program to top- and middle-level management. From their feedback, there will be directional input and feedback from top- and middle-level management to the facilities maintenance area.

The facilities maintenance program is in flux from the direction from management, the needs of the customers and building components, the performance of the work, the results provided from the customers, and further direction from management. The facilities maintenance team is the hub of the wheel of management that keeps the facilities maintenance wheel in motion. The customer's expressed positive results of the facilities maintenance program will keep the wheel from going flat!

IX

Epilogue

The goal of this book was to share my thirty years of facilities maintenance management experience with those who have the same career passion. I hope your time spent reading this book was rewarding and you found some points of interest that will be useful in your facilities maintenance management duties. I also wanted to open a dialogue on the best demonstrated management practices for a facilities maintenance program.

The takeaway statements from my thirty years of experience in facilities maintenance management are:

1. Facilities maintenance is extremely important.
2. Top- and middle-level management need to understand the broad implications of the need for a predictive and preventative facilities maintenance program as much as they do the business of making money and managing people.
3. A well-managed predictive and preventative facilities maintenance program, when evaluated against a "fix it when it breaks" program, is cost-effective and will provide positive results to the bottom-line—profitability.
4. A facilities maintenance professional is a major asset to the real estate department, assuring that the company properties are safe, operational, maintain the brand image, have a proper level of maintenance service, and ensure that the boss will have a positive experience with the company stores. All of this

accomplished from a coordinated and cost-effective facilities maintenance program.

5. The operations department, the boss, and the company brand desire the results of a predictive and preventative facilities maintenance program.

Top—and middle-level management want to make the right decisions. Our industry needs to present the facts and analysis to them that proves the take-aways listed above. This book is my contribution to this goal.

I'd like to thank my wife, Cathy, my daughter, Shannon Roberts, and my mother, Edna Robinson, for providing editing assistance.

Thanks go to Peter Mohrhauser, who requested that I prepare a presentation for vendor project management upon my retiring from Company A. It was this request that led me to write the management aspects involved in the entire process of facilities maintenance. This project allowed me to crystallize my thoughts of many of the management aspects that I utilized over my thirty years of management experience. I've enjoyed my relationship with Peter over the years we have worked together. Who better could I have chosen to write the foreword of the book? Thanks, Peter, for your kind words.

Thanks also to Timothy Christian, who encouraged me during this project, provided an idea for inclusion into the book, and helped me select a publisher for the book.

Thanks to Don Frankel and Rick McMasters who both read manuscripts of the book during its development, provided their thoughts and encouragement.

Thanks also to the WestBow Press team for their guidance, editing and developmental assistance in putting this book together.

Finally, I thank Jesus Christ, who certainly led me into this career and guided me all the way through it! He also led me into this book project and provided insight in its development.

X

APPENDICES

A. Al Tierney's Resume
B. Corporate Maintenance and the P&L Report
C. Parking Lot > $25,000 Project Process
D. Board-Up Process
E. Unit Codes Form
F. Projects and Spending Tracking Report
G. Capital Sub Budgets and Spending Report
H. Expense Sub Budgets and Spending Report
I. Projects Timing Performance Report
J. Life Cycle Maintenance and Repair Scheduled Tasks
K. Predictive and Preventive Maintenance Program:
    Real Estate Maintenance and Repair Schedule
L. Delivering Effective Facility Management

A. Al Tierney's Resume

CAREER OBJECTIVE
Provide facilities maintenance expertise to improve the services rendered by my clientele.

EDUCATION
Bachelor of Science-Civil Engineering, 1973; University of Dayton
Masters of Arts-Urban Ministry, 2004; Trinity Evangelical Divinity School

PROFESSIONAL EXPERIENCE
1/13-Present Tierney Consulting Services Company

President
Providing facilities maintenance expertise
al.tierney@att.net

8/02-12/12 Company A

Director of Facilities Maintenance
Developed the maintenance program that operates from unit code/unit cost principles and has as its goal to be predictive/ preventive in nature. Developed with staff assistance the network of national and regional vendors used to perform a large percentage of the work required.

10/00-4/02 Regal Alliance, Inc., Elk Grove, IL

President
Started this company to provide building construction and maintenance services for corporations.

7/81-10/00 Company B

Real Estate Manager

Responsible for the repair and maintenance of a nationwide network of sales counter/ warehouse facilities. Prepared the annual budgets. Managed the maintenance area staff. Managed the development of vendors used to perform needed repair and maintenance services.

4/80-7/81 Richard A. Miller & Associates, Inc.

Senior Associate

Responsible for the preparation of federal aid urban reports and engineering plans and supervision of subsequent construction. Involved in preparation of traffic studies, contract administration, financial coordination, and marketing.

10/78-4/80 P. R. C. Toups, Chicago, IL

Director of Engineering

Supervised professional staff in the preparation of municipal and land development engineering plans, specifications, estimates of costs, and bidding documentation. Responsibilities included contract administration, financial Coordination, and marketing.

6/76-10/78 Village of Carol Stream, IL

Village Engineer

Involved in reviewing engineering improvement plans, inspecting the subsequent construction, preparing and supervising the motor fuel tax program, designing municipal engineering improvements, and communication with the citizens and boards of the community.

4/73-6/76 Consoer, Townsend & Associates

Staff Engineer

Responsible for engineering design of municipal and land development projects.

Construction inspector and resident engineer on a $2,000,000 federal aid urban highway bridge project.

B. Corporate Maintenance and the P&L Report

An experienced facilities manager with long-term maintenance goals can relieve stress for store and district managers.

Al Tierney and Dave DiCarlo
Professional Retail Store Maintenance Magazine, April 2002

Though multisite regional and national companies spend enormous sums on brand building efforts, it's still common for customers to see obvious signs of facility deterioration when they enter a local store or restaurant.

There's a problem, but not with the facility.

Today many multisite companies burden the local store or restaurant manager with facilities maintenance decisions. Typically, all maintenance and repair expenses are bundled into a single line item in the loss column for the local store, restaurant or warehouse profit & loss statement. Since the manager's bonus is usually based on the location's overall profitability, maintenance costs that might unduly impact bonuses are easily deferred or given low priority. There's money to be saved, but not like this.

Corporate maintenance is much more complex than a single P&L line item would indicate, and it seems unreasonable to expect local managers to be qualified to coordinate and evaluate the performance of all maintenance and repair needs.

Corporate maintenance is really comprised of two separate concerns: custodial responsibilities and facilities management.

CUSTODIAL RESPONSIBILITIES

Custodial maintenance and repair work is the day-to-day housekeeping needed to properly run a business. These responsibilities range from general cleanliness, weekly landscape and lawn work, routine checks to ensure the site security systems and operating equipment are functioning properly and smaller repairs to the building's plumbing fixtures, parking lots and sidewalks. These building maintenance functions are nearly uniform for all similar locations and can therefore be included in the P&L report for each location. The store manager should budget for these expenses and they should be included in the company's annual budget. The district manager should monitor that the funds are spent by the store manager to assure that the work is performed. Because the work is uniformly needed at all similar locations and done on a day-to-day or month-to-month basis; these are temporary costs.

FACILITIES MANAGEMENT

Facilities management work effectively and efficiently preserves the esthetics, waterproofing, integrity and safety of the property, such as the landscaped areas, the parking lots, all sidewalks, stairs and landings and the building itself. Note: in all cases, the lease documents need to be reviewed to confirm responsibility so that the program can be tailored to meet specific requirements. Areas of concern for owned properties would include:

- ° Roofing—all roof maintenance, repair and replacement
- ° Plumbing—fire sprinkler systems, lawn sprinkler installations and underground utilities repairs
- ° Mechanical—all mechanical maintenance, repair and emplacement.
- ° Electrical—building re-lamping and maintenance, repair and replacement of electrical panels.
- ° Concrete—all major maintenance, repair and replacement.
- ° Asphalt—all major maintenance, repair and replacement and all parking lot sealing projects.
- ° Landscaping—all drainage and erosion problems.
- ° Exterior walls—all painting, weatherproofing, caulking and repairs.
- ° Interior materials—all floor, wall and ceiling finishes maintenance, repair and replacement.
- ° Environmental—all projects
- ° Structural—all repairs
- ° Remodeling—all projects

° Energy management—all projects
° Waste management—all projects

Facilities management is concerned about long-term investments and improvements to a location, including both expense and capital expenditures. It requires planning for long-term effects to maximize the life cycle of installed building components and take advantage of national and regional purchasing power. Also, because the age and components of each building vary, needed expenditures will vary as well.

Since there is no uniformity of maintenance work or costs within this maintenance category, these expenditures should be on a portion of the P&L report that would include fixed or untouchable company expenditures (except by upper management), such as corporate advertising, facilities management, etc. These funds are a necessary part of doing business and shouldn't be held hostage by annual bonus expectations.

Under this new approach, who would be best qualified to address the long-term planning concerns of this type of work and best able to ensure that the work is performed properly? The local store manager? The district manager? Or an experienced facilities manager?

CONSIDER THE ALTERNATIVES

Using our definitions of corporate maintenance, consider the following scenarios.

1. A facilities management program under the direction of an experienced facility manager who understands these issues and makes them priorities.
2. Store Managers and District Managers are unable to do so even in the best of circumstances, given all the responsibilities in running a profitable business.

Here are three sample scenarios;

1. Local Site—National Chain Restaurant: Roofing Issue

A. Store Manager/District Manager

Roof installation date was never recorded. Repairs and warranty period are not tracked. The roof is fixed only if it leaks. On a busy Friday night, the roof falls under heavy rain. The kitchen and seating areas are inundated with leaks. Customers run for cover and the kitchen is in disruption as buckets are located.

While a roofing company located in the Yellow Pages can fix the roof, it isn't available until Tuesday. They recommend a new roof membrane and what they call "the best product on the market." A contractor is found to repair the inside of the restaurant. They have no corporate specifications and will take their best shot.

RESULT: The restaurant has been damaged, business has been disrupted for days and customers inconvenienced. Cost is not an issue at this point.

B. Facilities Manager

The roof is inspected under a facilities management program. The type of roof and manufacturer is noted. All repairs are tracked, and the roof is evaluated every couple of years for needed repairs and to ascertain the remaining years of service that this roof membrane has.

Under this program, and extra 4 years of life can be gained from the roof. A replacement is planned and budgeted. A contract is negotiated with a roofing membrane manufacturer and the project is bid among three approved roofing applicators. The roof is replaced early in the budget year with little fanfare—and prior to failure.

RESULT: No disruption to business and the company saves at least $15,000 as compared to above.

2. **Local Site—National Retail Chain: Mechanical Equipment Issue**
   A. **Store Manager/District Manager**

   It's 98 degrees outside in Atlanta, on a hot day in July. At noon, the store is busy and one of two HVAC units goes down. The one remaining unit can only hold 85 degrees inside.

   Using the Yellow Pages, a mechanical contractor is found. They can only come the following business day. They recommend that the entire unit be replaced. The age of the unit isn't known, so it's replaced under emergency conditions.

   This new unit continues to break down regularly. The mechanical contractor is less than dependable.

   RESULT: Disgruntled customers, less business than expected and higher costs for emergency work.

   B. **Facilities Manager**

   The installation date of the unit is known. All mechanical equipment has been inspected twice a year under a contracted maintenance program. All repairs have been tracked.

   When the HVAC unit goes down, the maintenance program service company is called. They find that a contractor is malfunctioning. Since the unit is still under warranty, the repair is made immediately at no cost.

   RESULT: No loss of business and customers stay cool.

3. **Local Site—National Retail Chain: Exterior Walls Issue**
   A. **Store Manager/District Manager**

   The store in Milwaukee has painted block walls. The store is eight years old. The faded paint starts to peel and a mysterious white substance (efflorescence) covers a good portion of the walls. The manager thinks it should be painted. Bids are sought. The low bid is $10,000, but the second quarter has not been good and a $10,000 loss on the P&L report will make it look worse. Business gets better, time flies by and winter sets in.

   The manager goes back to the same contractor a year later to begin the painting project. The contractor reinspects the building and finds that there are mortar joint failures and a good bit of tuck pointing that needs to be done to allow for a proper coating of paint. Sand blasting is also recommended to remove peeling paint.

RESULT: Customers complain about the store exterior. New price is $25,000.

B. Facilities Manager

The building is under a facilities maintenance program. The lifecycle of the building's waterproof coating is 8 years, and it is now 8 years old. Because other stores in the chain have block walls, it's understood that they must be waterproofed properly because they are prone to rainwater penetration, which under the freeze/thaw conditions in Milwaukee could damage the integrity and useful life of the walls. An approved painting contractor familiar with the chain's southeastern Wisconsin stores performs this work.

RESULT: The walls are properly waterproofed under a negotiated rate with an established contractor. Customers compliment the store's appearance.

DIFFERENT PERSPECTIVES AND OBJECTIVES

An owner of a business or property is in it for the long term. They have major responsibilities that are key to the running of the business. A manager of a restaurant, store or warehouse has responsibilities to run the location's day-to-day business. They're not in the best position to make decisions about long-term facility issues. An experienced facilities manager is.

While it makes sense for site managers to be accountable for custodial responsibilities at their restaurants, stores or warehouses, it's unfair to expect them to perform the duties required of a facilities management professional. The customer's perspective of your business includes the appearance and maintenance of your facility. Marketing and brand building efforts bring customers into local restaurants and stores, hopefully to return. So the experience must be a positive one. A facilities management program can help ensure that it is.

To work, facilities management requires a proactive approach to building components' life cycles. That means replacing custodial thinking with a long term view.

a. Track each location's spending on the P&L report to ensure accurate costs, but facilities management costs should be on a portion of the report that includes fixed or untouchable company expenditures.
b. Put a qualified facility manager in charge of the facility management program, freeing site managers from decisions that can adversely affect their bonus expectations.
c. Develop a level-of-service desired for your facilities management program and a cost-per-square foot for this service.

Facilities benefit because they gain the ongoing attention they deserve from an experienced facilities manager. The corporation benefits because short-term thinking always costs more money, and that affects overall profitability. Building components last longer with life cycle and cost solutions, reducing replacements and emergency repairs. Customers will see the difference when they walk in the door.

When we wrote this article, I was the President of Regal Alliance, and Dave DiCarlo was the Midwestern Regional Construction Manager for Gateway Country.

C. Parking Lot > $25,000 Project Process

(Three bids and submittal of the $25,000 approval package)

A   RE Parking Lot Project Data and Request for Vendor Services Form—
    sent to vendor. RE FMPM enters project into computer system and
    will track progress of this project through completion.

B   Vendor performs a parking lot survey of this store's parking lot
    Site Visit #1
    Vendor fills out the "Vendor—Pavement Survey Form," proposal,
    and diagram; attaches photos; and sends these to the RE FMPM
    for approval.
    Included in the vendor pavement survey are the following:
    1.   Store location and contact information
    2.   Parking lot asphalt and concrete areas and number of
         regular and handicapped parking stalls
    3.   Pavement ranking
    4.   Drainage conditions review with the store manager
    5.   Drainage information: type, condition, and ponding on the
         parking lot and adjacent land
    6.   Photos taken during the pavement survey
    7.   Recommendation for type of parking lot improvement

    Included on the diagram are the following:
    1.   Store
    2.   Parking lot with number of parking stalls shown
    3.   ADA parking stalls and striping
    4.   Proposed patching with dimensions
    5.   Drainage patterns
    6.   Storm sewer piping and structures
    7.   Project phasing plan
    8.   Indication where photos were taken from
    9.   Legend for the proposed improvements

    Included with the vendor proposal are the following:
    1.   Vendor proposal

2. Detailed description of each paving and drainage improvement with quantity and unit measurement, unit costs, and total costs
3. Existing and planned layouts for the ADA handicapped parking stalls
4. Applicable details for the pavement project
5. Note: asphalt thickness needs to be determined for all capital improvement projects
   a. If asphalt is three inches or thicker, only core the asphalt thickness; if pothole exists, then get info from pothole
   b. If asphalt is fewer than three inches thick, core the asphalt and stone sub-base
   c. If pumping of sub-grade is evident, then a minimum five-foot-deep core is needed

C   RE FMPM reviews the survey, diagram, proposal, and photos and either asks vendor for additional information or submits to director of facilities maintenance (DFM) for her or his review and approval. If DFM approves, then the FMPM is advised, contacts the vendor, and asks the vendor to proceed with the three-bid process.

D   Vendor prepares the three-bid package and submits to RE for approval.
Included in the three-bid package are the following:
1. Three-bid tabulation (to be sent to bidders)
   a. Detailed description of each paving and drainage improvement with quantity and unit measurement
   b. Unit bid and total columns included for the bidders to fill in
2. Construction notes—state all important directions and information that the contractor will need to be aware of to properly price and perform the project
3. Diagram (revised to include core information)
   a. Showing the existing core locations and depths

      b. Showing the proposed cross-section for the planned improvements

  4. Cores

      a. Diagram showing the locations of cores taken and the existing asphalt thickness at each location

      b. Photo documentation showing the existing asphalt thickness at each location

  5. Existing and planned layouts for the ADA handicapped parking stalls

  6. Invoice for $1,200 for core samples

  7. Applicable details for the pavement project

E RE reviews the three-bid package

  1. FMPM reviews and marks up as needed any corrections or lack of information

  2. FMPM decides to send his or her review back to vendor for improvement or approves the project

F RE approval to solicit bids—FMPM e-mails vendor that the three-bid package is approved

G Vendor prepares the three-bid package to be sent to its selected three bidders

H Vendor submits bids to RE along with the invoice for the 60 percent of the project management fee

I RE FMPM prepares the $\geq$ $25,000 approval form and package for management approval of the project and the invoice for 60 percent of the project management fee. Both are then submitted to the DFM for her or his review and approval. Note that this should be just a cursory review, because the project was approved in step E above. Then the package and invoice needs to be reviewed and approved by the RE VP. If the project is over $50,000, it also needs to be reviewed and approved by the corporate controller or CFO.

J   RE FMPM issues vendor a purchase order for the project and the entire project management fee

K   Vendor and RE set up a pre-construction phone conference with the awarded contractor's representative, the store manager, and possibly the assistant district manager

L   Vendor provides project management for the construction phase of the project up to completion of the improvements, including at least one site visit (second work site visit)

M   Vendor approves the project construction and submits an invoice for the project and the remaining 40 percent of the project management fee, including a punch-out site visit (third work site visit)

N   RE FMPM closes out this project as follows:
1.   Calls the store manager to confirm that the work is completed and the project site is properly cleaned up
2.   Closes out the project in the computer system
3.   Issues invoice for approval to DFM

D. Board-Up Project Process

RE Board-Up: Vendor—Work Flow Process and Specifications

1. Store manager contacts vendor or FM project manager and notifies them of the need for a security board-up
2. FM project manager contacts the service provider (vendor)
3. Service provider receives call from the store manager or the FM project manager
4. Service provider determines the following:
   a. Store location
   b. Store manager's name
   c. Store phone number
   d. Area of and reason for the board-up
   e. Size of openings affected—doors and windows
   f. Magnitude of the damage and what ultimate improvements are needed
   g. Enters project into service provider project tracking software, noting time day and time received
   h. The subcontractor to be contacted to perform the needed improvements
5. Service provider contacts subcontractor's office
   a. All pertinent info from step 4 is relayed to subcontractor
   b. Subcontractor advised to expedite service, call in upon arrival, report extent of damage, take a photo of the existing conditions, advise if board-up can take place immediately or if materials have to be purchased, if materials needed state when improvements will take place, advise when the board-up is done, and take photo of completed work.
6. Subcontractor's office does the following:
   a. Dispatches work request to his or her technician
   b. Passes on the service provider's information and requests as stated in 4 and 5 above
   c. Advises the service provider of the technician's ETA
7. Service provider calls the store manager to advise her or him of the technician's ETA

8. Technician does the following:
   a. Introduces himself or herself to store manager
   b. Calls subcontractor's office upon arrival
   c. Reports back extent of damage
   d. Takes a photo of the existing conditions
   e. Advises if board-up can take place immediately or if additional materials are needed
   f. If additional materials needed, states when will improvements take place
   g. Advises when the board-up is completed
   h. Takes a photo of the completed work
   i. Advises what permanent improvements are needed as a result of the cause for the board-up
9. Subcontractor's office then follows ups as follows:
   a. Submit before and after photos with invoice
   b. Discuss the permanent repairs and/or replacements needed with the service provider
10. Service provider then contacts the FM project manager to discuss the following:
   a. The permanent repairs and/or replacements needed
   b. Before and after photos taken by the technician
   c. Invoice for the board-up submitted to the FM project manager and close out of the board-up project
   d. Contacting the store manager to do a follow-up phone survey to ascertain the level or service that was provided by the technician
11. FM project manager then does the following:
   a. Approves the invoice and closes out the board-up project
   b. Advises the store manager of any project to do repairs and/or replacements for permanent improvements

Board-Up Specifications

1. All first-floor windows and doors should have plywood covering the entire opening and frame. The covering should be secured with carriage bolts that cannot be removed from the building's exterior. Eliminate any potential safety hazard caused by any

interior protruding bolts used in securing the boarding. The use of nails or screws that penetrate the frame or mullion is prohibited.

2. All properties should be boarded in accordance with local codes. If local codes differ from these guidelines, local codes supersede.
3. Plywood thickness should be ½ inch thick for window openings and 5/8 inch thick for door openings. The plywood covering should be one continuous piece when possible.
4. Carriage bolts mated with nut and two flat washers (interior and exterior) are to be used to attach the plywood to the 2 x 4-inch boards. Washers should be large enough to fully accept the square portion of bolt beneath head.
5. Two-by-four-inch lumber should be used inside the doors and windows as the attachment point for plywood. These should be a minimum of sixteen inches longer than the width of the plywood cover. (Note that the 2 x 4-inch board will be drilled with ½-inch diameter holes that line up with the holes in the plywood covers.)

Replacement Glass

1. All glass windows should be replaced with tempered safety glass or laminate (sandwich panel) safety glass if approved by the FM project manager.
2. If a bay door window is broken and the glass can be replaced with laminate safety glass while on site for the initial call, proceed with the glass replacement. Otherwise, board-up the opening and quote replacement with tempered glass.

E. Unit Codes Form

0100 ROOFING

0100 Roof
0115 Gutter Sys
0120 Coping
0125 Roof hatch
0130 Roof flashing
0135 Smoke hatch
0137 Skylights
0140 Roof drains
0170 Coat Metal
0175 Canvas canopy
0190 Structural canop
0337 Roof hoods

0200 PLUMBING

0210 Fire Sprinklers
0211 Fire Pump
0220 Sanitary sewer
0225 Oil/Debris seper
0230 Storm sewer
0240 Septic tank 0375
0241 Catch basin/MH
0242 Dry wells
0245 Sump pump
0250 Water main/ser
0253 Wtr backflow
0254 Fire spklr backfl
0255 Water hydrant
0260 LR plumbing
0265 Water heater
0270 RR plumbing
0280 Water fountain
0295 Misc plumbing

0300 HVAC

0301 Gas Line
0305 HVAC service
0308 Salesroom
0309 Office
0310 Sales & Office
0315 Renovation
0320 Ductwork
0325 RR exhaust fan
0330 LR exhaust fan
0335 Shop exh fan
0336 Ceiling fans
0485 Building ground
0338 Vent Dampers
0340 Evap coolers
0345 Unit heaters
0346 Infrared htrs
0350 Thermostats
0360 Base elec htrs
Gas conversion 0510
0395 Misc. mechan

0400 ELECTRICAL

0401 Lamps
0402 Office lighting
0404 Shop lighting
0410 Building lighting
0413 Building lighting
0413 Exterior lighting
0415 Sign lighting

0400 ELECTRICAL(cont)

0416 Track lighting
0417 Lamp recycling
0418 PCB ballast dispos
0420 Electrical panels
0425 Computer cabling
0430 Shop electrical
0431 Office electrical
0432 Storage electrical
0433 Exterior electrical
0460 Security system
0480 Power poles

0490 Lightning repairs
0491 Emergency power
0495 Misc elec repairs

0550 HARDWARE

0501 Overhead doors
Metal passage drs
0516 Front entrance dr
0519 Windows
0543 Security gate
0595 Elevators
0546 Window bars
0548 Lexan windows
0560 Mezzanine stairs
0570 Railing
0580 Bollards
0590 Fencing

0600 CONCRETE

0605 Parking lot
0610 Conc pad
0615 Dumpster pad
0620 Curbing
0621 Conc whl stops
0625 Expansion jts
0630 Sidewalk
0631 Landing/steps
0635 Pressure clean
0640 Shop floor
0642 Shop floor jts
0650 Retaining walls
0660 Foundations
0675 Caulk sw/bldg
0695 Misc repairs

0700 ASPHALT LOT

0710 Parking lot
0711 Overlay lot
0715 Speed bumps
0720 Seal & stripe
0750 Drainage
0780 Restripe lot
0785 Handicap pkg
0795 Misc repairs

0800 LANDSCAPING

0810 Grass/sod
0815 Mulch/stone
0820 Plantings
0825 Weed control
0830 Drainage
0831 Retention pond
0835 Erosion control
0850 Trees
0860 Lawn sprklr sys
0870 Assessment
0880 Pest control
0890 Fire lane
0895 Misc repairs

0900 EXT WALL MATL

0910 Exterior walls
0915 Remove graffiti
0920 Seal brick walls
0925 Clean ext walls
0930 Exterior trim
0935 Rooftop equip
0940 Expansion joints
0945 Caulk winds/drs
0947 Misc caulk
0950 Wall materials
0951 Metal panels
0970 Efflorescence
0975 Tuckpointing
0991 Property inspect
0994 Misc painting
0995 Misc repairs

1000 INTERNAL MATL

1005 Salesrm flr VCT
1010 Office flr VCT
1011 RR flr VCT
1030 Salesroom walls
1045 Salesrm cabinets
1050 Lunchrm cabinet
1070 Ceiling tile
1071 Ceiling tile & grid
1075 Restrm partition
1095 Misc repairs
1096 Misc cleaning
1097 Painting

1100 STRUCTURAL

1100 Seismic repairs
1120 Foundation rpr
1125 Wall support rpr
1130 Roof Struct rpr
1150 Struct evaluated

1200 EXT SIGNAGE

1210 Wall-non illumin
1220 Wall-illuminated
1230 Tag line
1240 Reader boards
1250 Pole sign
1260 Ground level sgn
1270 Directional sign
1280 Misc repairs

ACTION CODES: F = Fix/Repair, I = Inspection, R = Replace

F. Projects and Spending Tracking Report

Note: This book format precludes the ability to show the Excel report capable of fitting on a single-page space, so I will list the headings. Hopefully, this will be understandable.

Headings:

Top line (separate columns):

1. Budget type
2. Zone or region
3. Expense
4. Tracking expense budget
5. Capital
6. Tracking capital budget
7. Totals

Second line (categories beneath line one columns):

3. Active, Complete
4. Dollars Committed, Budget, (+/-)
5. Active, Complete
6. Dollars Committed, Budget, (+/-)
7. Projects, Dollars

Third line (categories beneath the second-line categories):

3. Active—projects, dollars
3. Complete—projects, dollars, average days
5. Active—projects, dollars
5. Complete—projects, dollars, average days

Each budget type is shown in column one, with each zone or region having its own line to show data. Then the projects and dollars information is entered for expense and capital. Next, the tracking expense and capital information is filled in. Finally, the projects and dollars totals are entered for each zone's or region's budget type. At the bottom of the report, the totals of each column are shown.

G. Capital Sub Budgets and Spending Report
(As of the end of each month)

Note: This book format precludes the ability to show the Excel report capable of fitting on a single page space, so I will list the headings. Hopefully, this will be understandable.

Headings across the top:

1. Facilities Maintenance Sub Budgets
2. Actual Spent (completed)
3. Pending (active projects)
4. Maybe to 12/31 (Not completed or active projects—projects under consideration and historical spending trends)
5. Year-End Estimated Total Dollars to Be Spent
6. Budget for the Building Component
7. B/W (Better or Worse)

Headings down the facilities maintenance sub budgets:

1. HVAC
2. Roofs
3. Parking lots
4. Overhead doors
5. Signage
6. Special projects
7. General (other building components grouped together)

Your list of these headings will vary.

H. Expense Sub Budgets and Spending Report (As of the end of each month)

Note: This book format precludes the ability to show the Excel report capable of fitting on a single page space, so I will list the headings. Hopefully, this will be understandable.

Headings across the top:

1. Facilities Maintenance Sub Budgets
2. Actual Spent (completed)
3. Pending (active projects)
4. Maybe to 12/31 (Not completed or active projects—projects under consideration and historical spending trends)
5. Year-End Estimated Total Dollars to Be Spent
6. Budget for the Building Component
7. B/W (Better or Worse)

Headings down the facilities maintenance sub budgets:

1. HVAC
2. Roofs
3. Parking lots
4. Overhead doors
5. Signage
6. Lighting
7. General (other building components grouped together)
8. Electrical panels
9. Electrical branch

Your list of these headings will vary.

I. Projects Timing Performance Report

Note: This book format precludes the ability to show the Excel report capable of fitting on a single page space, so I will list the headings. Hopefully, this will be understandable.

Headings across the top:

Top line—separate columns:

1. Building Component
2. Average Days vs. Standard
3. Projects within Standard (completed projects)
4. Open Projects

Second line—categories beneath line one columns

2. Average Days to Complete
2. Standard Days to Complete
2. (B/W) (Average better or worse days)
3. Total Projects Completed
3. Projects Better than Standard
3. Projects Worse than Standard
4. Total Open
4. Total Late
4. % Late

Headings down the building component column:

1. Roofing
    a. Company   Repair
    b. Landlord   Repair
    c. Company   Replace
    d. Landlord   Replace
2. Plumbing
    a. Company   Repair

b. Landlord   Repair
c. Company   Replace
d. Landlord   Replace

3. HVAC
   a. Company   Repair
   b. Landlord   Repair
   c. Company   Replace
   d. Landlord   Replace

4. Electrical
   a. Company   Repair
   b. Landlord   Repair
   c. Company   Replace
   d. Landlord   Replace

5. Doors
   a. Company   Repair
   b. Landlord   Repair
   c. Company   Replace
   d. Landlord   Replace

6. Concrete
   a. Company   Repair
   b. Landlord   Repair
   c. Company   Replace
   d. Landlord   Replace

7. Asphalt parking
   a. Company   Repair
   b. Landlord   Repair
   c. Company   Replace
   d. Landlord   Replace

8. Landscaping
   a. Company   Repair
   b. Landlord   Repair
   c. Company   Replace
   d. Landlord   Replace

9. Exterior walls
   a. Company   Repair
   b. Landlord   Repair

    c. Company   Replace

    d. Landlord   Replace

10. Interior improvements

    a. Company   Repair

    b. Landlord   Repair

    c. Company   Replace

    d. Landlord   Replace

11. Structural

    a. Company   Repair

    b. Landlord   Repair

    c. Company   Replace

    d. Landlord   Replace

12. Signage

    a. Company   Repair

    b. Landlord   Repair

    c. Company   Replace

    d. Landlord   Replace

J. Life Cycle Maintenance and Repair Scheduled Tasks

Building Age—Four Years

1. Minor roof repairs
2. Miscellaneous plumbing repairs
3. Miscellaneous mechanical repairs—air movement units, heaters, HVAC units
4. Building relamp
5. Repair signs; check mounting, appearance, and electrical connections
6. Repair dock doors
7. Warehouse concrete floor repairs
8. Asphalt parking lot seal and stripe
9. Landscaping improvements

Building Age—Eight Years

1. Minor roof repairs
2. Miscellaneous plumbing repairs
3. Miscellaneous mechanical repairs—air movement units, heaters, HVAC units
4. Building relamp
5. Miscellaneous electrical repairs—breakers, panels
6. Repair signs; check mounting, appearance, and electrical connections
7. Repair dock doors and seals, man doors, front entrance doors, and double-swing doors
8. Concrete repairs—warehouse floors, dock slab, sidewalks, curbs, and gutters
9. Asphalt parking lot repair, seal, and stripe
10. Landscaping improvements
11. Exterior wall repairs
    a. Paint/seal block walls, brick walls as needed
    b. Recaulk expansion joints, metal to wall joints as needed

12. Interior remodel
    a. Finished office space—showroom, office, lunchroom, restrooms, training rooms, and management offices
        1) Replace carpet and rubber base
        2) Clean/replace acoustical ceiling tiles, grid, and grilles
        3) Sheetrock walls—repair and paint
        4) Wallpapered walls—clean, repair, or replace
        5) Clean windows inside and outside and blinds
        6) Improve wall finishes as required
    b. Warehouse area
        1) Paint warehouse block walls and sheetrock walls as required
        2) Repair wall and roof areas
    c. Restroom improvements as needed
        1) Update fixtures
        2) Repair/replace stalls, dividers
        3) Repair/replace plumbing apparatus—toilets, flushing devices, etc.

Building Age—Twelve Years

1. Minor roof repairs
2. Miscellaneous plumbing repairs
3. Miscellaneous mechanical repairs—air movement units, heaters, HVAC units
4. Building relamp
5. Miscellaneous electrical repairs—breakers, panels
6. Repair signs—check mounting, appearance, and electrical connections
7. Replace dock doors
8. Replace dock seals
9. Repair man doors, front entrance doors, and double-swinging doors
10. Concrete repairs—warehouse floors, dock slab, sidewalks, curbs, and gutters

11. Asphalt parking lot repair, seal, and stripe
12. Landscaping improvements

Building Age—Sixteen Years

1. Replace single-ply roof (Note: these were 40-mil ballasted or mechanically attached), major roof repairs to built-up roofs
2. Miscellaneous plumbing repairs
3. Replace HVAC units
4. Replace heaters
5. Miscellaneous mechanical repairs—air movement units
6. Building re-ballast and relamp
7. Miscellaneous electrical repairs—breakers, panels
8. Replace exterior signs
9. Replace double acting doors
10. Replace metal man doors
11. Repair dock doors, dock seals, front entrance doors
12. Concrete repairs—warehouse floors, dock slab, sidewalks, curbs, and gutters
13. Asphalt parking lot repair, seal, and stripe
14. Landscaping improvements
15. Exterior wall repairs
    a. Tuckpoint mortar where needed
    b. Repair wall cracks where needed
    c. Paint/seal block walls, brick walls as needed
    d. Recaulk expansion joints, metal to wall joints as needed
16. Interior Remodel
    a. Finished office space—showroom, office, lunchroom, restrooms, training rooms, and management offices
       1) Replace carpet and rubber base
       2) Clean/replace acoustical ceiling tiles, grid, and grilles
       3) Sheetrock walls—repair and paint
       4) Wallpapered walls—clean, repair, or replace
       5) Clean windows inside, outside and blinds
       6) Improve wall finishes as required

b. Warehouse area
1) Paint warehouse block walls and sheetrock walls as required
2) Repair wall and roof areas
c. Restroom improvements as needed
1) Update fixtures
2) Replace stalls, dividers
3) Replace plumbing apparatus—toilets, flushing devices
4) Replace mirrors

Building Age—Twenty Years

1. Replace built-up roofs; paint/repair metal roofs
2. Building utilities review
   a. Municipal utilities—sanitary and storm sewers and water main services
   b. Electrical service and grounding
   c. Gas piping and meter
   d. Fire sprinkler system
3. Miscellaneous plumbing repairs
4. Miscellaneous mechanical repairs—air movement units, heaters, HVAC units
5. Building relamp
6. Repair signs—check mounting, appearance, and electrical connections
7. Replace front entrance doors
8. Replace dock levelers
9. Repair man doors, double-acting doors, dock doors, and seals
10. Replace exterior concrete as needed
11. Repair warehouse floor
12. Landscaping improvements

K. Predictive and Preventive Maintenance Program

Real Estate Maintenance and Repair Schedule
(This was the first schedule to start this program.)

It is real estate's goal to meet or exceed the following schedule:

January: Annual Introduction

Real Estate will issue annual contracts and a list of the branches on the current four-year life cycle maintenance and repair program to the relevant area contractors for their particular territories.

January-April: Visit Buildings to Establish Scope of Work

Real estate alone, the area contractors alone, or both together will visit branches on the current four-year life cycle maintenance and repair program and develop the scope of work for each in accordance with the specific tasks for the life cycle year and the building's age.

March-May: Bid Submittal

Area contractors will submit proposals for the work to real estate.

March-June: Award Work

Based upon acceptance of the submitted proposals, real estate will issue work orders to the area contractors, authorizing them to proceed with projects.

March-September: Construction Season

Area contractors are expected to perform assigned work.

October-December: Establish Budget and Projects for the Following Year

Real estate and/or area contractors will begin to inspect buildings on the four-year life cycle maintenance and repair program for the next year and develop the scope of work for the upcoming cycle. Area contractors will commence to submit bid proposals for these projects.

L. Delivering Effective Facility Management

Al Tierney
Professional Retail Store Maintenance Magazine
December 2001/January 2002 and February 2002

Imagine walking into your favorite retail store or restaurant, and after navigating broken tiles in the outer lobby, you notice a patch of worn, grease-stained carpet near the restrooms. Inside, a bucket catches overflow from a loose faucet, and duct tape secures a few ceiling tiles damaged by a roof leak. As a customer, would you return?

Customer attitudes are perceptions about your facilities and are important. Unresolved maintenance and repair problems can impact customer perceptions of your locations and undermine their confidence in your brand image. These perceptions affect your future sales and profits.

So why are many multisite locations' maintenance and repair needs being neglected? How important are these issues to consumer shopping, dining, and buying decisions? What practices and methods are in place today to address ongoing building maintenance needs? Why do many of these practices fail? Is there a better way?

First and foremost, organizations with multisite buildings must understand that maintenance and repair of those buildings is an important and necessary part of doing business and ensuring customer brand loyalty. Many current practices, while ensuring short-term profits at the local site level, may actually undermine an organization's marketing and customer strategies and its overall corporate sales and profits.

This article briefly outlines some of the most detrimental current practices, attempts to quantify their impact on the bottom line, and provides a road map for a predictive and preventative maintenance program (PPMP). Such a program, managed by a professional facility manager, can help national, multisite organizations streamline and improve the facility maintenance and repair process, ensure better service to the properties and site managers, and help reinforce and sustain customer confidence in the corporate brand.

Importance of Facility Maintenance to Customers

How important is the maintenance of your facilities to your customers? For most customers, it is the top priority.

Many practices in place at multisite corporations fail to give facility maintenance and repair the same priority or importance. While marketing and sales efforts are increasingly more customer-centric, facilities practices and programs have not kept pace. Many practices relegate facility maintenance to an afterthought rather than view it as an important part of encouraging and sustaining customer loyalty.

Current Maintenance and Repair Practices

Cost-effective maintenance of national/regional multisite retail stores, wholesale outlets, and warehouse facilities has always challenged facilities staff, operations, accounting, and finance departments—both on a daily basis, as building components need repair and replacement, and yearly during the budget cycle.

Fast-growing, expanding organizations are focused on new buildings. Consequently, maintenance and repair issues have a lower priority. Facility maintenance and repair practices created during that growth and expansion may not be effective, as business cycles change and buildings age when planning and budgeting challenges become more dramatic and apparent. As infrastructure breaks down, employee and customer safety issues increase. As appearances become worn or outdated, the location becomes a less-than-desirable shopping or working environment.

Change is inevitable, though. As the economy tightens and business strategies shift from expansion to consolidation, current maintenance and repair practices must change. Many of the most common current practices take too great a toll on the organization and result in higher maintenance costs per square foot, unnecessary expenses, and lowered consumer confidence in your corporate brand.

Old-Style Thinking

Why do many national multisite organizations fail to give facility maintenance and repair the priority their customers want? The fact is that many corporations continue to use old-style facility maintenance practices. These maintenance and repair practices actually undermine many of their most impressive customer-focused marketing strategies. And ultimately, that costs more for maintenance and repair as well as new customer acquisition programs.

The old style of maintenance needs to be exposed for what it is— backward and incapable of doing an effective or efficient job. It costs more, wastes manpower, and doesn't address the life cycle issues of the building components. It is also confusing within the corporation, because there are many cooks in the kitchen, and it is frustrating to your facility manager, because she or he can't do the job she or he wants to do.

Inherent Conflicts of Interest

Today, many of the largest multisite chains rely on decentralized facility maintenance and repair. They budget dollars and track costs in each site's profit and loss analysis, investing site managers with responsibility for upkeep and repair.

Such a strategy may look reasonable on a P&L statement and appear to push decision-making for maintenance and repair to local managers, but often, it creates unexpected conflicts of interest. These can impact the overall life span of the facility and potentially undermine shopper confidence in the corporate brand.

For example, many site managers are evaluated and given performance incentives based on site profitability. In this case, costly replacement or repair work will often be deferred or simply not done in order to improve a quarterly P&L. Over a period of time and successive quarters, deferred routine maintenance can result in even more costly emergency service and eventually in customer dissatisfaction with the store or site experience.

The site's profit and loss analysis and the manager's bonus pressures affect decisions about the site's maintenance needs, creating a direct conflict of interest with an effective facility maintenance program (FMP). Clear, precise, and cost-effective decisions about the physical site take second priority to a potential profit-based bonus.

Considering the total dollar value of all of an organization's locations and the maintenance dollars spent per square foot, this old-style practice wastes resources, duplicates efforts, and costs much more than an effective, value-added FMP managed by a facility manager.

"Fix It When It Breaks" Philosophy

Often, a belief prevails throughout the organization that it's less expensive to fix building components when they break. After all, there may be many months or years of use before a building component breaks down. With an overriding focus on profits, organizations—particularly at the site location—often see routine maintenance costs for functioning building components as expendable, short-term savings to the bottom line.

Most routine maintenance—what could be categorized as three thousand-mile oil change procedures—is designed to sustain a building component's working life, helping to neutralize the effects of daily wear and tear. A "fix it when it breaks" philosophy, however, responds at the end of the component's life cycle. In some instances, repairs may be useless, requiring premature replacement of the building component.

When site managers view maintenance as costs that can be deferred to raise short-term profits, the "fix it when it breaks" philosophy becomes, in effect, a license to kill building components with neglect. By waiting for something to break before spending, organizations inadvertently shorten the life cycles of their building components and create disruptions in business as emergency repairs take place. Simply put, this wasteful and disruptive practice costs organizations more per square foot for building maintenance than necessary.

Marginalization of the Corporate Facilities Manager

Today, most multisite organizations lack an effective corporate facilities management program and an effective leader—a facility manager invested with strategic responsibility and decision-making authority. This is a surprising practice, considering the total value of an organization's locations and the cost per square foot for maintenance across all its sites, which can range from $1 per square foot for multisite wholesaling operations to $10 per square foot for major restaurant chains.

Increasingly, there's a growing belief that anyone can mange maintenance and repair work. After all, the burgeoning do-it-yourself industry, with its books and television programs, makes it look easy. Consequently, corporations delegate major decision-making responsibilities to site managers and operations departments and transform the corporate facilities manager into a day-to-day detail person who ensures that projects are completed and contractors are paid.

Internal Policies and Barriers

Internal corporate policies and entrenched attitudes within the facilities management team create barriers to an effective corporate facility management program (FMP), undercut the importance of facilities maintenance and repair to the financial health of the organization, and impact customer confidence in the corporate brand.

Barrier 1:—Mistrust of contractors and vendors. Relationships with contractors, service providers, engineers, and consultants are extremely important to controlling costs and sustaining a high level of service. Rather than viewing contractors as partners in the maintenance and repair process, in many organizations, an "us versus them" mentality prevails—a battle of wills. In an effective FMP, contractors become partners. These contacts are expert resources who stay knowledgeable about advancements in building components, specifying the appropriate installation details and maintaining uniformity of improvements.

Barrier 2:—Bid everything. Eighty percent of building maintenance improvements are routine and involve common replacement and repair items. Often, corporate policies, like bidding out every job, make facility management programs ineffective and inefficient. For example, since unit costs for these items are standard, prices can be retrieved easily in advance or updated quickly as needed.

Old-Style Maintenance ("Fix It When It Breaks") vs. Predictive and Preventative Maintenance

Fix It When It Breaks	Predictive and Preventative
100% breakdown and emergency	70% predictive maintenance
	15% preventative maintenance
	15% breakdown and emergency maintenance

<u>Benefits</u>

1. Perception that it saves money
2. Perception that it maximizes profits at each store procedures and materials

1. Life cycle awareness of all building components
2. Value engineering for work
3. Uniform procedures and maintenance levels across company locations
4. An enterprise-wide maintenance management database to track building component products repairs
5. An effective FMP that manages maintenance and repair expenditures to a cost per square foot of all the buildings being maintained
6. An approved and managed team of area contractors, service providers, engineers, and consultants that conforms to work quality, service levels, cost competitiveness, and trustworthiness standards

7. Annual contracts for area contractors and service providers, allowing for quicker response for approvals of work and more accurate budgeting

8. Frees operations staff and local store managers from major building-related concerns, allowing them to concentrate fully on sales, customers, and the business

9. Negotiated regional and national building component replacement parts contracts, generating cost savings and decreasing emergency purchase situations

Fix It When It Breaks vs.	**Predictive and Preventative**
Drawbacks	
1. Lack of strategy or plan to ensure budget maintenance dollars are applied effectively	1. Perceived loss of control of operations department and store managers
2. Premature aging and decommissioning of building components	2. Perceived increase in maintenance costs in the short term as the FMP is
3. Improperly maintained initiated building appearance and operational equipment	
4. Disruptive emergency repair projects that affect productivity and customer perceptions	
5. More frequent emergency work	
6. Lack of coordinated purchasing of building component replacements	
7. Lack of uniform appearance of multisite company locations diminishes the corporate brand	
8. Risk of health and safety issues that affect your staff and customers	

An effective corporate facilities management program (FMP), managed strategically by an experienced facility manager (FM), can transform old-style maintenance and repair practices. It can

- increase the life cycles of building components, decreasing unplanned capital expenses
- control maintenance costs per square foot

- set a strategy to address building maintenance concerns on an ongoing basis
- create the right atmosphere in top organizational levels for cooperation among other different departments
- ensure the appearance and operation of buildings, decreasing health and safety concerns
- add value and reinforce customer brand loyalty by giving maintenance for each corporate site the priority it deserves

What Is an Effective Corporate Facility Management Program?

An effective FMP provides the strategic management of an organization's valuable components—its business—and profit-generating buildings. It ensures that building components and their associated costs are managed from the moment they are installed. In effect, the FMP manages the expected life cycles of the components and applies the ongoing maintenance they need to function as close to new as cost-effectively and possible.

How does the FMP accomplish these goals and deliver benefits? By reengineering a "fix it when it breaks" maintenance program into a predictive and preventative one. With a predictive and preventative maintenance program, you will have

- a five-year budget schedule for a maintenance and repair program
- an understanding of workloads for the upcoming budget year six months before the budget year begins
- project plans and descriptions available for prices or bid before the budget year begins
- projects awarded early in the budget year, ensuring that outside work gets started as soon as weather permits
- significantly fewer surprises when visiting field properties
- increased savings on maintenance and repair projects
- significantly reduced emergency projects

How Is an FMP Managed?

An effective FMP adds value when it is under the direction of a qualified facilities manager who understands the strategic focus of the FMP and brings expertise to the process. The FM addresses the maintenance and repair needs of the entire organization, understanding site-specific needs as well as the overall business strategy of the organization.

The FM works with the operations, accounting, construction/real estate purchasing, and legal departments to service the needs of the multisite managers but has decision-making authority. The FM is the organizational expert in maintenance and repair with budget approval by corporate management.

Benefits of a Corporate Facility Maintenance Program

The end result of an effective FMP should produce a reliable maintenance cost per square foot for all buildings in an organization. Specifically, an effective FMP will

- create a more reliable, accurate budget and manage costs more effectively by scheduling a building component replacement program.
- reduce individual site replacement costs by establishing national or regional replacement building component purchase agreements
- reduce unanticipated component down time and attendant safety and health issues by establishing an orderly procedure to replace components before their anticipated failure date
- reduce or consolidate vendors, enabling greater control, efficient management, and greater cost savings.

Other corporate areas have maximized their purchasing power through vendor consolidations. With FMP, the same results can be achieved in maintenance and repair.

The FMP Budget

Budgeted dollars for the FMP should be a bottom-line expenditure within the annual operations department budget rather than be tied to each site's profit and loss analysis. An accounting improvement like this enables

- value-added life cycle of building components awareness
- implementation of maintenance procedures that increase life cycles of building components and decrease emergency situations
- implementation of corporate maintenance software that tracks building component data and maintenance and repair history
- cost savings through national and regional material and service provider contracts
- a predictive and preventative FMP

The FMP Seven-Step Roadmap

Once an FM staff is established and proper corporate authority and management are assigned, an FMP program can begin. In brief, an effective FMP requires tools, information, and cooperation.

1. Create a maintenance and repair responsibility table that is developed with input from the operations department. This table cross-references each building's components with the required maintenance and repair duties, assigning responsibility to the FM staff and/or the onsite staff at each location. FM staff assumes all responsibility for national or regional vendors, including vendor interviews, preparing requests for proposals, and awarding the work. For example, some building components need to be handled only by the FM staff to facilitate repair tracking so it is easy to determine when replacements are needed. These components include roofing, mechanical, electrical, hardware (doors, dock equipment, signage), and exterior walls. Components with minor repair or maintenance issues should be managed by the onsite staff.

A dollar amount can be set for their involvement, and the operations department would establish this budget.

2. Gather basic information about corporate field properties. This information includes the total square footage of the buildings grouped by facility type, the ages of the buildings, and annual expenses and capital expenditures for each building type.

3. Establish facility maintenance benchmarks. Using the square feet and spending information, you can determine your current annual cost per square foot for maintenance and repair for each building type. This becomes the FMP benchmark. Once determined, the FMP benchmark enables you to begin the budgeting process.

4. Capture the unit costs for repetitive maintenance and repair work. The FM staff can begin capturing this information from the performed repairs and replacements projects. This information gives you the unit costs for maintenance and repair work done at your facilities.

5. Develop the FMP budget. The FM staff develops a budget using the maintenance and repair responsibility table and its understanding of building component life cycles; selected contractors, service providers, engineers, and consultants; annual contracts in place for preventative maintenance; and the problems faced in the field, why they develop, and how to repair them.

6. Develop a list of preferred contractors. Using this information, you can begin to develop a preferred list of area contractors, service providers, engineers, and consultants for a range of projects. By consolidating your list of vendors, you establish partnership relationships with vendors who can help you maintain a consistent level of service and performance with both routine and emergency projects as they arise and become expert resources in their building component specialty.

Area contractors are general construction companies that have proven themselves in the following categories: service level, quality of work, competitive prices, and trustworthiness.

They service your sites in a clearly defined regional area of the country.

Service providers are companies that turnkey specific and recurring building component improvements, such as mechanical equipment, relamping, fire sprinkler systems, signage, and finish space flooring material companies.

Working with proven companies that know your specifications, expectations, and local managers is a big plus for all concerned. Their service levels, quality of work, costs, and trustworthiness have been approved and are welcomed each time you call them. Reusing these known companies will reduce time wasted soliciting bids, retraining new companies to your way of doing things, and surprises during the project. Also, enough projects awarded in this manner could very well alleviate the need for additional staff.

It is recommended that you develop a network of area contractors, service providers, engineers, and consultants that is the smallest number of companies needed to provide you with top-quality service and response. Depending on your needs, only a handful of area contractors should be necessary. For example, one Fortune 200 company uses only ten contractors to service 380 sites across the US.

One- to three-year contracts can be issued to selected area contractors and service providers. These contracts can have two two-year extension options included as well. When a work proposal is received, it can be approved with a work order or purchase order, speeding the receiving and awarding of work proposals to ensure that the work is performed on a timely basis.

7. Standardize maintenance and repair work. As the FMP is implemented, FM staff will become familiar with the recurring maintenance and repair projects they perform. This information enables them to develop specifications for these projects using value engineering principles that consider both the life cycles of the work procedures and materials and their associated costs. These specifications dictate work procedures

and the materials to be used, ensuring consistency in work and materials across all company sites and promoting corporate brand consistency as well.

Major capital projects that reach a certain dollar threshold and/or are intricate in nature should be put out to bid after the plans and specifications have been prepared. Typically, these projects don't have high reoccurrences, and it is best to use qualified companies that are selected by your architect, engineer, or consultant to bid on and handle them.

A Case Study in Predictive and Preventative Maintenance

A Fortune 200 corporation with 7.5 million square feet of space in 380 locations across the US wanted to gain greater control over its growing maintenance costs. Operating on a "fix it when it breaks" maintenance philosophy, the company found it was unable to predict its maintenance costs over time and encountered an increasing number of expensive emergency repair and replacement projects, while other maintenance projects lacked consistent standards, methods, or materials across the sites.

The company set out to transform this piecemeal process into a more streamlined, predictive one that was built on unit costs and focused on life cycle awareness of building components. It wanted to be able to develop a five-year budget and plan, reduce emergency maintenance calls, and save costs.

The first challenge the company faced was to be able to predict as much maintenance as possible. To do this, the facilities team listed all routine maintenance and repair tasks for each building component and the life cycle duration in years of each task.

Like the maintenance recommendations supplied by car manufacturers, the FM team understood that every building component, under assumed usage conditions, has its own life cycle. While car components need servicing after each recommended mile increment, the FM team determined that every building had a maintenance cycle of four years and a renovation cycle of eight years. Other task groups were also identified, including potential emergency projects that did not fall into either cycle, additional capital components, and preventative tasks.

From this information, the team established eight budget items as follows:

1. Four-year maintenance
2. Eight-year renovation cycle
3. Roofs
4. Parking lots
5. HVAC
6. Signage
7. Unpredictable emergency projects
8. Preventative maintenance, including HVAC, dock levelers, fire sprinklers, pest control, etc.

Each project was also prioritized into one of three categories—must do, should do, or would like to do—that allowed both the management and FM team to evaluate the strategic importance of each project to the site, the business, and its impact on customer perceptions.

Results of the Case Study

While the five-year budget provided a complete predictive picture of the projected work, its most important result was to calculate a per square foot cost for expense and capital dollars spent per the total area of all the stores. This critical benchmark enabled the FM team to work more effectively with corporate management and quantify its value to the organization.

Over time, the company realized significant benefits from its predictive and preventative program, including

- reduced emergency projects
- more efficient and controlled bidding processes. Knowing what projects were scheduled in July prior to the next budget year enabled the team to seek bids and pricing for the work prior to the next budget year.

- more efficient awarding of projects. Since most projects were predictive, the team could award the work in February, March, and April, gaining priority on the contractor's schedules and reducing project costs by up to 15 percent over late summer awards.
- reduced disruptions at each site. All of the needed work could be scheduled with site managers in advance and performed all at one time by an area contractor familiar with corporate policies and requirements.
- maximized building component life cycles, reducing replacements
- strategic oversight and management. Corporate management put the main responsibility for the FMP with the facilities manager and the FM team, freeing operations staff and locations managers from these time-consuming hassles.
- maximized cost controls through national and regional leverage. National and regional pricing agreements could be established with a handful of vendors, standardizing the materials used, increasing construction communication, establishing an expert resource for future projects, and saving costs.
- developed technology and tools to manage the program. The team developed a corporate maintenance management software system for project management to track projects and enable more effective building component repair/replacement decisions.

Old-Style Maintenance Exposed

Many of the largest multisite retailers, restaurants, and warehouse-based corporations invest millions in establishing their buildings and enticing customers inside. They spend millions each year to maintain their facilities. Yet, surprisingly, most have no strategic program in place to manage or control the maintenance and repair process in a way that supports and accommodates their business objectives.

When organizations use old-style maintenance practices or have "fix it when it breaks" philosophies, they spend almost as much as a predictive and preventative program would, but they are left with incredible amounts of deferred maintenance. The effects are wasteful and disruptive to the bottom line and to customer perceptions about the corporate brand.

By implementing a predictive and preventative maintenance program—a corporate facilities management program that is managed by a professional facility manager—you develop a knowledge base about your buildings, their components, and the best way to maintain them. The FMP enables strategic, business-oriented thinking based on component life cycles. It enables you to benchmark maintenance costs, quantify savings, and more accurately measure the impact of maintenance and repair on the bottom line.

An effective FMP provides better service to your properties, site managers, and customers. This type of facilities management program means you will better manage your maintenance and repair expenditures and keep your buildings and properties in the condition that you and your customers want.

When I wrote this article, I was the president of Regal Alliance. Note that in retyping this article some eleven years later, a couple changes were made.